THE GREAT RESET VS THE GREATEST REVIVAL

By

ANDRE DELAGE

PROISLE PUBLISHING

The Great Reset VS. The Greatest Revival

Copyright © 2022 by Andre Delage

ISBN: 978-1-959449-25-6

All rights reserved. No part of this book may be reproduced or transmitted in any form or by any means, electronic or mechanical, including photocopying, recording, or by any information storage and retrieval system, without permission in writing from the copyright owner.

FAIR USE NOTICE: Citations may contain copyrighted material, the use of which has not always been specifically authorized by the copyright owner. Fair dealing for the purpose of criticism or review does not infringe copyright if the source is mentioned: Sections 29, 29.1 of the Copyright Act of Canada create the fair dealing exception to copyright. The book content is the opinion of the author only with no Christian denomination affiliation. In this book, the author focuses on the Canadian Church's dismal spiritual condition and its non-partisanship in the Canadian political sphere.

Unless otherwise initiated from another version. All scripture is taken from The Open Bible Expanded Edition: New King James Version

Copyright © 1985, 1983 by Thomas Nelson. Used by permission of

Thomas Nelson. www.thomasnelson.com.

"Taken from the HOLY BIBLE: EASY-TO-READ VERSION © 2014 by Bible League International. Used by permission." "ERV" for the Easy-to-Read Version in English appeared at the end of every quotation.

The views expressed in this work are solely those of the author and do not necessarily reflect the views of the publisher, and the publisher disclaims any responsibility for them.

To order additional copies of this book, contact:
Proisle Publishing Services LLC
39-67 58th 1st Floor Woodside
New York, NY 11377, USA
Phone: (+1 347-922-3779)
info@proislepublishing.com

PROISLE PUBLISHING

Table of Contents

My Statement of belief - "THE WHOLE BIBLE" 1

To The 2022 Modern Church – just as the church at Laodicea was, so are churches of today 2

To my fellow brothers and sisters in Christ 2

"Our Darkest Days Are Ahead of Us" 4

God's judgment during the Covid-19 pandemic 5

Canada's institutions were conquered by treachery 7

Coup D'états 13

Truckers Freedom Convoys 18

Who dare questioning the authorities? 20

What is coming soon? 30

Believers Are Salt of the Earth, ... 33

A Light on a Lampstand 33

Christianity is not limited to the four walls of the Church Building 35

The Church of the Laodiceans 39

The Greatest Revival 39

Canadians Rejected God 41

Christians Rejected Knowledge, the Truth 41

The Rise of the Romanists 46

The Rapture 64

Until then, keep busy sharing the gospel as if it will be 50 years from now 64

DO YOU GET THE POINT? 66

But what about our nation, what can we do? 67

Remember for whom our veterans fought for 73

Last Call... 77

Doesn't Jesus consider us as friends?.. 81

Charitable Tax Exemption - A compromise with the devil ... 84

The reality check-.. 85

We are against the greatest cult... 85

Example of past concession 88

Duties of a member of the body of Christ..................................... 92

All deck on hands 92

Duty of Pastors 95

The Doctrine of the Rapture - Hindering the duty of a steward 96

What is Satan after, after all?...101

Why should it matter? 104

The Deceiver at Work 105

Signs of Wonders..108

God Delusion vs. Satan's Deceit..111

Modern Technology is Magic..118

Message to Pastors and Ministers...121

Admonition to the Modern Era of the Western Laodicean Nation Churches 127

The Greatest Revival is Starting Now with You..........................132

Conclusion 136

Final Word...137

To the left behind 144

Appendix 147

About the Author

The author is a Christian, a Canadian, who loves this country Canada. He loves God's Church, and mostly he loves his children and grandchildren. He is concerned about their future. In this book, he focuses on the Canadian Church's Laodicean spiritual condition that leads to the kidnapping of The Canadian Charter of Rights and Freedoms. He concluded that the Church's vulnerability within the political scheme of the federal government and provincial government is due to a divided Church and a falling away from the inerrancy of God's word. He is not a theologian, he is not a minister, and he does not hold any master's degree. His only desire is to share what he learned through studying of God's word.

He was born and raised in the Roman Catholic tradition, the Romanist culture. At age twenty, he purchased a Bible from a door-to-door solicitor "knocking at the door" and that is when he received the love of the truth. From that time on, he went through life looking for an understanding of God's word.

"I am a Canadian, a free Canadian, free to speak without fear, free to worship God in my own way, free to stand for what I think right, free to oppose what I believe wrong, free to choose those who shall govern my country. This heritage of freedom I pledge to uphold for myself and all mankind."

-Honourable John G. Diefenbaker leader of the Progressive Conservative Party

PREFACE

The Holy Spirit dwells in each believer, (1 Cor 3:16). The Church is the Holy Temple of God where His Spirit resided, (Eph 2:20-22). When the Church lives in the truth, it acts as a restrainer. The Church's responsibility is to restrain the mystery of lawlessness that is increasing and to prevent it from getting out of control.

Satan's plan is the creation of a one-world government, a one-world religion, the establishment of a new world in disorder, the Tower of Babel reincarnate. If you believe that this present immoral condition is bad, wait until the Church is removed, it will be like the day of Noah, the pre-flood period, and even worse.

> *"But God has chosen the foolish things of the world to put to shame the wise, and God has chosen the weak things of the world to put to shame the things which are mighty,"*
> 1 Cor 1:27

> *"If God is for us, who can be against us?"* Romans 8:31

Acknowledgement

My Father in heaven, My Lord and King Jesus, and The Holy Spirit The Comforter

My Statement of belief - "THE WHOLE BIBLE"

Notification

I use a book titled, "The Great Controversy," by E.G White, for reference on historical reform, notwithstanding his view on eschatology which does not reflect my views.

"Federal law allows citizens to reproduce, distribute or exhibit portions of copyrights motion pictures, video tapes, or video discs under certain circumstances without authorization of the copyright holder.

This infringement of copyright is called "Fair Use" and is allowed for purposes of criticism, news reporting, teaching, and parody."

My research also consists of verifying the accuracy of interpretation with the KJV Strong's Concordance.

To The 2022 Modern Church – just as the church at Laodicea was, so are churches of today

To my fellow brothers and sisters in Christ

The content of this book is for you, Christians who bear the name of The Way, (Acts 9:2,14), The Truth, (John 8:31-32) and The Life, (1 John 1:2), (John 14:6). Who believe Jesus is Lord, (Rom 10:9), - the Son of God is God (1 John 4:15) - not falsely known as only a historical figure, not falsely known as an angel, not falsely known only as a prophet, not falsely known as a spiritual being created by God, not falsely known as a simple man begotten by Joseph, but rather truthfully known as the Living God. His name is 'Father' who sent His Son in the form of a man. His name is Jesus (John 14:11, Rev 1: 4b-5a), born from a young virgin woman named Mary, (Matt 1:23). She married and became the wife to a man whose name was Joseph, her husband (Rom 3:23, Matt 1:20,24) and who bore many children (Luke 8:19, Mark 6:3).

A Christian is one who believes in the testimonies presented by the Apostles through generations to our generation, (John 17:20). A Christian is one who believes that Jesus died without sins, (1 John 3:5) and redeemed us by His blood (1 Jn 1:7, Rev 1:5) from Adam's curse and from the consequences of all our sins which condemned us to eternity in hell, (Rev 22:3, Mark 3:29). A Christian is one who believes in Jesus and His bodily resurrection followed by His ascension to heaven (Luke 24:51) where Jesus our Lord is seating at the right-hand side of God the Father, (1 Peter 3:22). A Christian is a man/woman of faith, who believes without evidence, (Gal 3:11), confesses with his/her mouth the Lord Jesus and believes in his/her heart that God has raised Him from the dead, therefore he/she is save, (Romans 10:9). A Christian is one who trusts in the inerrancy of the Bible, God's word is true, (Rev 21:5). A Christian is one who is called to be at one with God, (John 6:65, John 17:21-22). And finally, a Christians is one who is appoint to the works befitting repentance, subsequently steward of Christ revealing God's mystery. (Acts 26:20, 1 Cor 4:1, Col 1:26).

"Our Darkest Days Are Ahead of Us"
(U.S. President Joe Biden)

Jesus said, "I am the light of the world. He who follows Me shall not walk in darkness but have the light of life."

In my book titled, "Canadian Christian Ministry 2018 - The Most Lukewarm Church in The Whole Western Nations," I made a bold statement:

Christianity is my religion, my faith, and my belief, and the Canadian Charter of Rights and Freedoms protects me.

But first…

The just, the righteous one in the Church must first live by his/ her personal faith, Trusting in the Word.

Institutions and human beings will fail you.

But God will never, never fail you, (Zephaniah 3:5)

God's judgment during the Covid-19 pandemic

It felt like being persecuted but make no mistake we were judged according to our nonparticipation in the political arena of this nation Canada within the last four decades.

The Apostle Peter stated that judgment starts with the Church.

> *"For the time has come for judgment to begin at the house of God; and if it begins with us first, what will be the end of those who do not obey the gospel of God?"*
> 1 Peter 4:17

It is my view that Canadian churches were placed under God's judgment during the Covid-19 pandemic as was the nations. The Charter of Rights and Freedoms was challenged and abused in all aspects of our lives. IT FAILED TO PROTECT the believers and unbelievers alike.

The Charter of Rights and Freedoms is not a privilege. The Charter of Rights and Freedoms is a constitution, an institution that is the supreme law in Canada. It recognized the Supremacy of God. The Charter of Rights and Freedoms failed to protect our rights to make choices during the unfounded pandemic mandates. We are now in the year end of 2022, and much has changed since I published the book in 2018, it has become worse. The government not only has complete control over the education of our children but also of our Christian Religious Gathering" within our church building, regarding restrictions on the number of people allowed in the building at one assembly. The church building is no longer respected as a sanctuary[1]. Below you will see the ruling made by the Superior Court of Justice. Ruling on the Constitutional Validity of Religious Gathering Restrictions (Covid-19).

According to a ruling by ONTARIO SUPERIOR COURT OF JUSTICE, The Honourable Judge Renee M. Pomerance stated, quote

Section [173],

> "Hence, I have little hesitation in concluding that, while numerical and percentage gathering limits infringed s. 2(a) of the *Charter*, the salitary benefits of these restrictions outweighed the deleterious effects on religious freedom. Ontario has met its burden to establish that the regulations in issue are reasonable limits, demonstrably justified in a free and democratic society."

And then he, (the judge) criticized the respondents in these words in section [172]

> "I accept that this is a legitimate aspiration. However, it does not change the outcome in this case. I note, by way of digression, that, by breaching the law, the claimants showed a lack of respect for state authority. Their disobedience is, for constitutional purposes, beside the point. What does matter is the respect shown by Ontario to religious institutions by tailoring restrictions and easing them when it was possible to do so. Full accommodation of religious freedom would not have resulted in "legitimate inconvenience" for the government. It would have rep-

---

[1] https://www.jstor.org/stable/48648345?seq=10#metadata_info_tab_contents

resented a wholesale abdication of government responsibility to act in the public interest. It would have meant turning a blind eye to the threat of severe health consequences for a large swath of the population."

The whole verdict can be viewed on this web link, Ontario v. Trinity Bible Chapel et al, 2022 ONSC 1344 (CanLII)

Will it be appealed to the Supreme Court of Canada? It has not been announced yet.

Canada's institutions were conquered by treachery

In the Canadian Charter of Rights and Freedoms, section 1 says that all rights in the Charter are protected subject to reasonable limits. This does two things: (1) it guarantees all rights in the Charter; (2) it provides an approach to the limitation of the rights. In Canada, once a right has been violated in a law, the burden shifts to the Government to prove that the violation is a "reasonable limit, prescribed by law in a free and democratic society. This requires that the government show, with evidence, that there is: (1) a pressing and substantial objective served by the law that limits the right; and (2) that the right is proportional.

Canada's institutions were conquered by treachery[2]. Since the government is corrupt, it is guaranteed that Canadian Churches have lost their rights and freedoms. The Covid-19 virus has not been proven to be called a pandemic. This is not a covid-19 conspiracy theory, but a conspiracy in the truth. I invite you to watch "Doctor Kelly Victory who is explaining everything about covid-19" video posted on July

---

[2] https://rumble.com/embed/v1pl00m/?pub=gi6jj

7th, 2020, that has been removed for violating YouTube's Community Guidelines, uploaded on rumble.com,[3]
Have the covid-19 death related statistics been tampered with? Did the news medias report effectively the government statistics? The newspaper obituary shows no increase of death rate compared to previous flu season years. Ask a Funeral Service Manager. Time will prove that the pandemic was orchestrated to fulfill the United Nations agenda 21. What is agenda 21? Agenda 21 is a non-binding action plan of the United Nations with regard to sustainable development. It is a product of the Earth Summit (UN Conference on Environment and Development) held in Rio de Janeiro, Brazil, in 1992. Believe it, Covid-19 was meant to further this diabolic vision to bring the entire world into a totalitarian state. It is all about control of your conscience, our will, self-determination and all your material belongings with absolutely no discrimination. Your right to life is almost gone, your right to travel is almost gone, right to privacy is gone, there is surveillance cameras everywhere, and everything you say is recorded, your bedroom TV is a spyware device. Alexa on your cell phone is an electronic spy agent. Invasion of your privacy is a crime, yet telecommunication industries, web browsers, television networks, all social networking website, and financial institutions get away with it. Why, because you consent to give it away. To receive service of some kind with the bank, credit financial institution, or store online, in exchange you must agree to their terms or conditions, or else the service is denied. All free software you download comes with a condition to share your information with a third party. Nothing is free. All activities, pictures, opinions, and your whereabouts on social media are shared.

Next is Agenda 2030. What is Agenda 2030? On 25 September 2015, the 193 countries of the UN General Assembly

---

[3] https://rumble.com/embed/v1pl00m/?pub=gi6jj

adopted the 2030 Development Agenda titled "Transforming our world: the 2030 Agenda for Sustainable Development".

According to Wikipedia, https://en.wikipedia.org/wiki/Sustainable_Development_Goals

> The 17 SDGs are: No poverty, zero hunger, good health and well-being, quality education, gender equality, clean water and sanitation, affordable and clean energy, decent work and economic growth, industry, innovation and infrastructure, Reduced Inequality, Sustainable Cities and Communities, Responsible Consumption and Production, Climate Action, Life Below Water, Life On Land, Peace, Justice, and Strong Institutions, Partnerships for the Goals.

Agenda 2030 will control all land, all water sources, all resources, minerals, plants, energy, animals, all construction, and all food, its means of production, all information, and all humans. It is about controlling population growth. The three pillars of the U.N. agenda 2021 are Ecology, Economy, and Equity, (EEE). You will own nothing and be happy… the perfect utopia. The same propaganda tactic was used against the German Jews. The Luciferian elites are after your freedom of conscience, they want to take away the truth of who you are, and that is you are a creation made in the image of God. Watch this plan being publicly revealed titled, "The Great Reset | COVID-19 BEAST System Explained"[4].

---

[4] https://rumble.com/embed/vz59je/?pub=gi6jj

Covid-19 pandemic mandates, its restrictions, and forced mandatory vaccines are a crime against humanity and against God. These restrictions created huge unnecessary hardship on all aspects of the population[5]. Many citizens think that these drastic measures were a power grab scheme to control the population, a precondition for the elite's New World in Disorder. Deliberately bringing to bankruptcy thousands of businesses, unjustified death of elders with no one by their side, malnourished elders without personal care, an increase in depression among elders and teenagers, an increase in suicide among them, loss of jobs, therefore loss of revenues to whoever refuses the jab, consequently no allocation from EI (employment insurance benefit), many drawn from their savings and many more living on credit until the inevitable, declaring bankruptcy, leaving their family home and neighbourhood.

In October of 2021, the federal government announced that anyone travelling by air, train, or ship, must receive the required number of Covid vaccines to travel. The travel ban prevented approximately 6 million vaccine-free Canadians (15% of Canada's population) from traveling within Canada and prevented them from flying out of Canada. Canada's new definition for vaccination required boosters could double or triple the number of affected Canadians should the travel mandate be renewed in the future. On June 14, 2022, the Federal Government issued a news release, announcing that as of June 20, the vaccine requirements would be suspended "for domestic and outbound travel, federally regulated transportation sectors and federal government employees." Shortly after, the Federal Government filed a motion with the court seeking to strike out the legal challenge because the Travel Ban was no longer in force. The Justice

---

[5] https://rumble.com/v19fpzn-watch-james-topp-met-with-mps-in-person-for-over-an-hour-today-to-have-an-o.html

Centre filed its response to the Federal Government's motion, "this travel ban has not been canceled, only suspended, and so court action must continue," notes Ms. Chipiuk, therefore a Travel Ban lawsuit is in the process. Source: Justice Centre for Constitution Freedom[6]

It as been a very tough time for parents. Lockdown caused mental health in children who were forced to live in small living areas. Hard on the homeless who were deny a meal from the many soup kitchens that imposed mandatory vaccines. So many other hardships, included pastor was fine for giving food to the homeless such as Pastor Artur Pawlowski[7], many pastors who defied the mandate by keeping their church open were heavily fined and some were arrested[8]. The fear of a pseudo-pandemic was greater than the love for our neighbour, (2 Timothy 3:2-5). These are all signs of a takeover from our Canadian government that acts similar to a communist tyrannical government.

All political parties are part of the Great Reset Agenda.

For a brief description of the Great Reset please view this video title, "The Great Reset" by Dr. Gene Kim[9].

The corruption is much bigger than you can imagine. The mentality and moral behaviours are equivalent to if not, much worse than Nazism. These elites do not care. If you are not part of their group, you are less valued than an animal. The atrocities made toward the Jews are remarkably similar. It all started with a campaign of propaganda under the ruse

---

[6] https://www.jccf.ca/
[7] https://thefreethoughtproject.com/be-the-change/covid-19-homeless-pastor-fined
[8] https://www.thestar.com/news/canada/2021/02/21/church-whose-pastor-was-arrested-for-defying-covid-19-restrictions-holds-service.html
[9] https://youtu.be/2Xwilhs6Ou8

that it is for our own benefit. Isolating the Jews for their own protection in ghettos was a tactic to control herds moving in a particular direction in one location, ready for slaughter. These self-appointed elites do not care. Their attitude of superiority surpasses the average person. They are modern pharaohs, the new world in disorder, Caesars - both heads of state and the religious leaders. Lucifer is their leader promising all what their perverted hearts desire. They also have been deceived by Satan's lies, (Revelation 12:9).

These people think that they own the earth, that we are a plague on the earth needed to be controlled. The irony of this is that they honestly believe they are right. For some they have been deceived and for others it is a choice to reject God as so many will at the end of the thousand years reign of Jesus as King of the earth, (Rev 20:8). They are extremely demonic individuals who have pleasure in making life miserable. In their eyes, you are only a herd of cattle.

The bible states that there are many anti-christ, all having the characteristic of the anti-Christ to come. Please read my commentary titled, "Personality and Characteristic of the Little Horn Referred to The Anti-Christ[10]"

Canada does not have a nationalist party that would represent the interest of Canadian sovereignty. It is incomprehensible to see that 80% of the population failed to recognize the lies and deceptions.

---

[10] https://www.simplicityinthegospel.com/2019/05/personality-and-characteristic-of.html

Coup D'états

Coup D'états & the Plot to Steal America, Canada, and the Western Democracy[11]

It is a coup d'état that was in the making over two thousand years ago. In 1960, President J.F. Kennedy warned the American people. Do you know what transpired for revealing the elite's plot that infiltrate all government institutions? It was his execution.

Few are aware that Lord Mountbatten was approached by the Bank of England Co. and associates, led by Cecile King, chairman of The Mirror Group News Paper, (Ref: S3.E5 Coup, The Crown TV Series)[12]. They asked Lord Mountbatten to assist them to subjugate the British government. The elites were not incredibly happy with the present government policies to devalue the British pound. That meant an overwhelming loss for the Banks (elites' investment). Mountbatten responded that he would investigate the enactment of a coup d'état, but he was exposed and rebuked by Queen Elizabeth. She explicitly instructed him to mind his own business and to let democracy take its course… to do nothing.

He did an in-depth study about what successful world insurgencies had in common. Lord Mountbatten shared his assessment with the frustrated insurgent. This is what I will share with you, the conclusion of his research about the viability to overtake the Great Britain government and how it has been implemented in Canada and elsewhere in the free world. He explained.

---

[11] https://rumble.com/embed/vnyykq/?pub=4
[12] https://www.historyextra.com/period/20th-century/lord-mountbatten-did-prince-philip-uncle-attempt-lead-coup-harold-wilson-government-crown-true/

A successful insurgency consists of 5 elements.

- Control of the media
- Control of the economy
- The capture of the administrative target for which you need the fourth element
- Loyalty to the military
    I. Secured parliament
    II. Whitehall
    III. Ministry of Defense
    IV. The Cabinet Office – which includes the Prime Minister
        - i) To implement shutting down of the airport
        - ii) Train station
    V. Imposing a Curfew - thru a Martial Law declaration
    VI. The control over the police authority nation-wide which required tens of   thousands unquestioningly loyal servicemen

Now, the fifth element, the one and the most indispensable element – is legitimacy, the long-established institution required to support the coup d'état.

It consists of

- The Court, the body of Common Law, and The Constitution. For any action against the state to succeed, you must overthrow these as well as he explained.

Yet there was an obstruction, and as Lord Mountbatten explicitly explained, in the highest evolved democracy such as Great Britain, their authority is sacrosanct, (regarded as sacred and inviolable). That is why a coup d'état in Great Britain does not stand a chance, he stated. Unless, as he explained, they had the support of the one person not yet mentioned. 'The Crown,' has at its disposal unique constitutional power. The Queen could dissolve Parliament and appoint a new government and Prime Minister.

The Queen is also Commander in Chief of the Armed Forces. They swear allegiance to her and not to Parliament. The Sovereign holds the title 'Defender of the Faith and Supreme Governor of the Church of England'.

Since the Queen did hear thru the Prime Minister Harold Wilson about Mountbatten being approached by the Bank of England & Co. Lord Mountbatten's coup d'état has never been put into action, demonstrating at that time the power and authority of the Queen - like a Caesar.

Surprisingly, these individuals have never been charged with treason, but they kept the plot. It never occurred to me that the elites would use this plot for the takeover not only of Great Britain but also of all the western nations, the symbol of democracy and freedom. These individuals are better known as the 'secret societies,' namely the Cabal, the elites, and its puppets, the Illuminati, the Shriners, the Freemasons, the Jesuits, the Knight of Columbus, Skull, and Bones, and many more. There are about sixteen secret societies all playing a role to control the world. They are today all in the open, portrayed as the good Samaritans (the deliverers of the environment and the protector of Covid pseudo pandemic). They are the authors of the new normal promising the citizens of the world a new utopia, free of debts but owning no property, in the so-called New World In-Disorder.

This is the same propaganda used to herd the Jews for slaughter.

Who is the man leading the great reset agenda? Klaus Martin Schwab is a German engineer, economist, and founder of the World Economic Forum. Yuval Noah Harari who is a lead advisor for Klaus Schwab. What is Yuval's view of the future? It is to create a brain computer interface, to create a single collective society of humanity. I am not joking. The Borg of the Star Trek Voyager series sci-fi will become reality in fifty years. Watch Yuval Noah Harari comment,

https://rumble.com/embed/v19n7v9/?pub=gi6jj

At the very top are the Luciferians who have rejected Jesus as Lord but instead have accepted Satan as a lord with his destiny in hell for eternity. What motivates Lucifer to bring chaos to humanity? Satan will never be what we human beings are, created in the image of God with the destiny to reign with God for eternity to whoever accepts Jesus as Lord. Satan knows his destiny, which is hell for eternity. Lucifer hates human beings so much that he wants to bring in hell as many of God's creatures created in His image for eternity, (Prov 28:15, 1 Pet 5:8). Lies and deceit are his weapons of war. These so-called secret societies are victims of Satan's trickery. These self-appointed elites believe that Satan is the victim who was misjudged and mistreated by God.

> *"So, the great dragon was cast out, that serpent of old, called the Devil and Satan, who deceives the whole world; he was cast to the earth, and his angels were cast out with him,"* Revelation 12:9

As Lord Mountbatten explained, for a successful coup d'état, the Queen must be an active participant. The only way that this could be achieved is to create an event that would persuade the Queen that there is an imminent threat to the population. These elites created a pandemic, a pseudo-pandemic. Unfortunately, I suspect that the Queen was compromised, therefore she also has been played. With King Charles at the thrown now, nothing will stop them in achieving their goals.

In Canada, the Bill of Rights is the biggest obstacle to the elites' plot. The Canadian Bill of Rights Assented on August the 10th 1960, An Act for the Recognition and Protection of Human Rights and Fundamental Freedoms. There was an attempt to replace the Bill of Rights by The Charter of Rights and Freedoms as part of the Constitution Act, 1982 which relinquished the authority of the Queen to Canadians. The Charter never did receive royal assent nor received acceptance by all the provinces. The province of Quebec never did sign the Constitution Act since it caused it to lose its right of veto. The 1960 Bill of Rights still applies today. Yet, well cover-up. Only the Proclamation of Patriation was signed by the Queen in 1982. That is the date that we officially were supposed to become Canadian citizens and cease to be a British subject. As of this day, we are still British subjects. Canada is still a colony. Many attempts were made to add Quebec to the Constitution… Remember the Meech Lake Accord? The Accord proposed strengthening provincial powers and declaring Quebec as a "distinct society." It failed. Therefore, this made The Charter of Rights and Freedoms void, (supposedly). To know more in detail, please go to Canadian Peoples Union website [13]; https://www.thepowershift.ca/about

You may ask, "But what is so wrong and dangerous about the Charter?" It created the biggest loss of rights in one clause. It adds a condition that gives all powers and authorities to Parliament.

---

[13] https://www.thepowershift.ca/about

Truckers Freedom Convoys

There was a glimmer of hope during the Truckers Freedom Convoys where thousands of Canadians were cheering for them on overpasses along the highway en route to Parliament Hill. They were coming from all regions of Canada in the hope of being heard by our government and bringing an end to the unnecessary mandates. It was unsuccessful.

The Truckers Freedom Convoys and participants were disrupted by an unjustified brutal police force who acted upon the government's unfounded Emergencies Act. The participants were declared terrorists. The law was used to "strengthen police powers to impose fines and imprison people; compel tow-truck companies to help clear blockades; allow banks to freeze the personal and corporate accounts of individual protesters without a court order.

I do not single out only the Hon. Prime Minister Trudeau's government. All parties were in collusion and are guilty of crimes against humanity. The Conservative party now under the flag of supporting the oppressed were totally in support of Trudeau's Covid-19 policies by giving a blank cheque and by not opposing and questioning any of the restrictions on covid-19 health statistics. Only a few MPs spoke out. They were quickly dismissed and thrown out of their party.

"Ottawa Police Officer, Helen Grus was facing a charge of Discreditable Conduct after investigating unexplained deaths of children with potential links to the Covid 19 vaccines. As part of the SACA (Sexual Assault Child Abuse) unit, their mandate is to investigate all sudden and unexpected child deaths of children under the age of five. These investigations are crucial and mandated by law." Ottawa Police Officer, Helen Grus was suspended from her duties. But may have her suspension rescinded, according to her lawyer[14]. A reputable retire policing officer friend explains that unexplained deaths are first investigated by a provincial coroner or other such legal authority. If the deaths are suspicious, then the coroner would explain why and the manner of death in detail before a police investigation is launched as a criminal matter.

Although Ottawa Police Officer, Helen Grus was conducting "a private investigative project" which she had no authority to investigate in the first place, there is no more further investigating on the increase of the unexplained deaths of children under the age of five. And on the subject of death of children under the age of five, there has been also an increase of stillborn in Canada. Would that be related to the covid-19 vaccine[15] [16]?

A must watch; Dr. William Makis Crime against Humanity
https://rumble.com/embed/v1u41fq/?pub=gi6jj

---

[14] https://canoe.com/news/local-news/suspended-detective-accused-of-seeking-links-between-child-deaths-and-covid-19-vaccines-set-to-return-to-work-lawyer-says-but-ops-says-no-timeline-has-been-set/wcm/a5f2f9d3-1eca-4f4c-8450-44c3631bbff7
[15] https://www.worldtribune.com/alarm-sounded-on-increased-incidence-of-stillborns-reported-among-vaccinated-mothers/
[16] https://rumble.com/embed/v1u41fq/?pub=gi6jj

Who dare questioning the authorities?

Here is a list of individuals and organizations who spoke out against government-ordered mandates and restrictions intended for COVID-19.

- Maj. Stephen Chledowski serving member of the Canadian military
- Sixteen United Conservative Party MLAs spoke out against their own government's move to impose more stringent public-health restrictions
- Randy Alexander Hillier served as a member of provincial parliament in the Legislative Assembly of Ontario, funder of the No More Lockdowns organization.
- Derek Sloan MP was kicked out of the Conservative Party caucus and represented the riding of Hastings—Lennox, and Addington. He raised concerns about the censorship of doctors and scientists as well as medical information related to vaccines. Dereck Sloan is now the leader of The Ontario Party.
- Maxime Bernier founder and leader of the People's Party of Canada. Formerly a member of the Conservative Party,
- Pastor Artur Pawlowski, now leader of the Independence Party of Alberta , Laura-Lynn Tyler Thompson interview Pastor Artur[17]
- Pastor Tobias Tissen,
- Pastor Tim Stephens,
- Pastor Henry Hildebrandt and assistant Pastor Peter Wall
- Laura-Lynn Tyler Thompson

---

[17] https://rumble.com/embed/v1t4oo0/?pub=gi6jj

- Pastor James Coates
- Joel Lightbound, the Louis-Hébert, Que. MP stepping down as the chair of the Quebec caucus
- Warrant Officer James Topp who publicly spoke out against federal vaccine requirements while in uniform and charged
- Dana-Lee Melfi, popularly known as "Peace Man" during the Ottawa freedom convoy,
- Number of health experts and medical professionals such as.
- Dr. Mike Yeadon,
- Dr. Paul Alexander
- Dr. Crystal Luchkiw
- Dr. Steven Malthouse
- Dr. Chris Shoemaker
- Dr. Mark Trozzi
- Dr. Rochagne Killian
- Dr. Holly Fourchalk
- Dr. Charles Hoffe
- Dr. William Makis MD, https://gettr.com/user/makismd
- Constitutional Lawyer Rocco Galati
- Sarah Miller, Human Rights Lawyer
- Nichole Bourassa - Canadian People Union
- Tamara Lich - known for her involvement in the Canada convoy protest in Ottawa
- Pat King - known for his involvement in the Canada convoy protest in Ottawa
- Tom Marazzo - Freedom Convoy Participant
- Candice Malcolm - Founder of True North
- Officer Erin Howard who stood by her oath to uphold the Charter
- Justice Centre for Constitutional Freedoms

- Suzanne Coles- Speaks at the Waterloo Region Freedom Rally
- Jordan Peterson - a Canadian media personality
- Brian Peckford - a Canadian politician
- Rebel News, the only trusted Canadian news media
- A large group of Mennonites
- Thousands of federal public servants were put on a leave of absence refusing the mandatory vaccination rules, including myself.
- Thousands fired or put on unpaid leave of absence including thousands of workers who refused to get COVID-19 shots imposed by their employers
- 10,000 unvaccinated health care workers across Canada have been placed on unpaid leave or had their jobs terminated by health authorities
- Lest we forget the thousands of heroic truck drivers and their supporters who took a stand against mandatory vaccines and against the 14 days of quarantine at the US and Canada border. The support was so great, that over ten million dollars was contributed to the causes but were declared illegal and an act of terrorism by the Federal government
- Police on Guard for Thee, https://policeonguard.ca/whistleblowers/
- Dr. Patrick Phillips Family @ Emergency Physician
- Svetlana Dalla Lana - Canada Health Alliance -
- Scarlett Martyn – Paramedic
- Kim Sonmore – Paramedic
- Canadian Peoples Union website; https://www.thepowershift.ca/about
- Vaccine Choice Canada - https://vaccinechoice-canada.com/
- First Freedoms Foundation https://firstfreedoms.ca/
- First Freedoms Foundation https://firstfreedoms.ca/

- Watch this video presented by The Justice Centre for Constitutional Freedoms presents "The Convoy that United the Country [18]," https://rumble.com/embed/v1df691/?pub=gi6jj
- Many unknown Christians who prayed daily for justice and righteous leaders to intervene in support of the HELPLESS, THE POOR, MISSING CHILDREN, TEENAGERS, ELDERS IN SENIOR HOMES, AND THE WIDOWS.

The Tiananmen Square Massacre on June 4th, 1989 is a reminder of what is to come upon Canadian freedom. Now on July 1st, 2022, the Canada Day celebration on Parliament Hill was at its minimum. No access to Parliament Hill was allowed to protesters. There were many blockades and inspections en route to Parliament Hill. There were exasperating fines for many minor infractions, which have viewed as an all acts of intimidation from the government police force. Only a few who made it to express their opinions were scrutinized by the mainstream media distorting any view opposing the government. This is not Canada, the land of the free, when the government fears its citizens and by all means quench the truth within a peaceful protest, even within a celebration. Canada's democracy had fallen[19].

This summer (2022), we enjoyed a temporary reprieve from the pandemic mandate. In the public sector, the non-vaccinated employees were allowed to go back to work, and the mask mandate has been removed in major part, yet there are many insecure victims of the lies who are still wearing masks in public, even outdoors and in cars… go figure. Many are

---

[18] https://rumble.com/embed/v1df691/?pub=gi6jj
[19] https://www.simplicityinthegospel.com/2020/04/the-plot.html

still voluntarily being tested even though they have no symptoms, and if found positive for covid-19 wear a mask and confine to stay home. It seems to have become normal. But it is not. There is an economic depression luring and a new Covid variant. The effect of a recession is upon Canadians. The price of goods has increased, mostly due to the devaluation of the dollar due to an unlimited amount of money borrowed during Covid-19. The more money is printed the more the value of the dollar decreases. Consequently, the interest rate increase. A surtax on gasoline and diesel has been implemented for protecting the environment which also contributes to the inflated cost of living. Alberta oil production has been reduced due to government policies… a political ruse to cripple the economy via protecting Mother Earth. She is so powerless that she needs the magic of politics, surely not science to help her. Climate change is only a ruse to impoverish Canadians.

This nation of Canada is under God's judgement. "Under An Act of God." So many are blaming the government of all levels, all parties, and even blaming the war in Ukraine for our demise. Many Canadians are so gullible, easily believing the mainstream media. The media have received millions of so call bailout money so that government could control the air, after all, Satan is the prince of the power of the air, the spirit who now works in the sons of disobedience[20][21]. So many believe the cause of the continuous health crisis is the unvaccinated.

Yet, many Canadians cannot hit the nail right on the head to know the true cause of our degenerating national illness. It

---

[20] https://www.rebelnews.com/exclusive_news_media_who_secretly_took_trudeaus_61m_pre-election_pay-off
[21] https://www.canadaland.com/canadian-media-liberals-trudeau-government-funding-covid-cbc-erin-otoole/

is due to our sinful nature and unwillingness to live according to God's righteousness, and His instructions. It looks so hopeless. Chickens are too dumb to do anything stupid, while sheep follow any leader without asking questions. Whether you are a Christian, or an atheist, Satan is after God's creation made in His own image. He is after God's family nucleus. Destroy the family, and God's plan is interrupted. Satan always targets the children to disrupt God's purpose to procreate in a family structure.

> "I have met Justin Trudeau three times," said Pastor Steve Long, a Canadian Baptist minister. "Sadly, my last meeting with him in his office was very disappointing. He told me that evangelical Christians were the worst part of Canadian society[22]."

Canada instituted 'pride day' for the full month of June to celebrate a perverted lifestyle that goes against God's intent for a man and a woman. Through Hon. Justin Trudeau's government, the age for anal penetration has been lowered to 16 years old. Sex with animals is allowed in Canada, as long as there is no penetration, (go figure). Drag Queens are allowed to influence children in our schools. Parents allow their children to be bystanders in a pride parade with all its depravity. In the 1970s Unitarian congregations in Canada blessed same-sex relationships and worked to promote equal rights for gay men and lesbians. Same-sex marriage supporters include the Metropolitan Community Church, Canadian Anglicans, and the United Church of Canada. Transgenderism just as homophiles have deliberately attempted to confuse the terms "sex" and "gender" and use them interchangeably, to confuse our young children at school. The government accepts this lifestyle, promotes it, and imposes laws to protect

---

[22] https://www.ipcprayer.org/ipc-connections/item/11834-canada-justin-trudeau-christians-worst-part-of-society.html

this perverted life choice without the consent of the parent. Fifty thousand children in Canada per year disappear and rarely return home, 460,000 Missing Children in the USA each year. And lest we forget, 947,365 abortions were performed between 2011 to 2020 in Canada. There is no law to protect the unborn. Abortion is legal anytime during its pregnancy, from conception to the last moment of the 9th-month pregnancy. You wonder why God allows this to happen. God is gracious and merciful, slow to anger, (Joel 2:13). Surely there is no God you say, (Psalm 14:1). Remember God gives us freedom of conscience, the freedom to do good or bad. To obey or disobey. God did not give freedom to sin evermore without consequences. All have sinned and have fallen short of the glory of God. Being lukewarm and staying on the fence is one of the causes of our national demise. To the unbelievers, *"There is no fear of God before their eyes,"* Romans 3:18

> *"So rend your heart, and not your garments; Return to the Lord your God, For He is gracious and merciful, Slow to anger, and of great kindness; And He relents from doing harm,"* Joel 2:13

Freedom of speech has become intolerable in Canada, and freedom of conscience has been banned. Satan wants to remove our freedom to decide, to make a choice to accept God as the creator. Is it fair to send someone to hell if he/she does not know the truth about his/her origin of life, of who he/she is which is a creature made in the image of God, and to choose who to follow for eternity? There are parents that will let their children decide when they grow up. Decide what? To follow their footsteps, which is the only alternative the child has, there is no choice.

Satan wants to hide the truth of God being our Father. Satan wants humanity to believe that they have no father, that humans come out from the goo to the zoo, to people.

Canada has become a pilot program for condemning free speech... freedom of conscious. If the most democratic and free speech country of the world fall, all other nation will follow. The radical left is the extremism, their strategy is to accuse their opponent of extremist – pure Marxist strategy propaganda with the goal to destroy the constitution and the rule of law. They create an atmosphere of distrust toward any who have a different view other than their own.

> "In time of universal deceit, telling the truth is a revolutionary act." George Orwell

You can be put in prison for telling the truth, you can mistakenly disappear, and be murdered for exposing the truth. When that starts to happen, it is a sign of an extreme dictator regime.

There are Canadians who have been treated as political prisoners who rot in jail on minor charges of mischief. One is an award-winning Canadian freedom fighter, Tamara Lich, who was taken into custody on June 27, after allegedly violating bail conditions imposed by an Ontario judge for her participation in the Freedom Convoy protests that rocked Canada's capital of Ottawa for nearly three weeks in February, has now been released. Pat King, a minor participant in the February Freedom Convoy protests, who has been falsely characterized as one of the core leaders of the protests by Canada's mainstream media was incarcerated on minor mischief charges since Feb. 18, 2022. Pat King has been released also since. Please read a summary of The Canada Freedom Convoy 2022[23], titled; "Canada Has De Facto Political Prisoners".

The Prime Minister of Canada has the supreme authority to govern the country of Canada. He can legislate any unlimited

---

[23] https://westandunited.cloud/canada-has-de-facto-political-prisoners/

law without interference and any obstructions from any opposition if any. The Prime Minister of Canada is more powerful than the President of the United States of America. The President of the United States of America to legislate any new law, requires the approval of the House of Representatives and the Senate. Without the House of Representatives and the Senate's approval, the President is idle, dead in the water. But now the abuse of executive orders has become Law in the Oval Office. That also shows the high influence control by the elites in American politics.

As long as the Prime Minister of Canada has the majority in the House of Commons and his Party Members of Parliament give their full support, the Prime Minister of Canada reigns supreme.

And when the majority failed, the Liberals and New Democrats simply entered a so-called confidence-and-supply agreement that saw the NDP supporting the Liberals. NDP Leader Jagmeet Singh, who may be described as the prime minister's political fortress of solitude, the protector of the reign of Jagmeet. His political ideology is communism under the guise of socialism representing the working class. It falls right into the globalist communist agenda.

There is no stopping Prime Minister Trudeau until 2025, unless he voluntarily steps down. The only obstacle that could have been used in the past was the Canadian Charter of Rights and Freedoms. Yet of late The Charter has failed to protect its citizens. A Ruling on Constitutional Validity of Religious Gathering Restrictions (Covid-19) has proven that the government actions were justified in clause 1.

> *"The Canadian Charter of Rights and Freedoms guarantees the rights and freedoms **set out in it subject only to such reasonable limits** prescribed by law as can be demonstrably justified in a free and democratic society."*

As of now, all Canadians are treated as political opposition, knowingly or not. If you dare to speak against their policies, you are accused of radical extremist, and hate crime. This government political restriction has become a population activity control as in communist nations. There are many immigrants from communist countries such as Eastern Europe and North Korea, who chose to come to Canada that can testify to this assertion. How bad is communism? Billions have died under communist regimes[24].

According to Patricia Adams, Canada, a country of 38 million, has 6 million political prisoners, the number of partially vaccinated or unvaccinated Canadians that the Trudeau government has prevented from boarding a plane or boat to leave the country.

Canadians have no voice in politics to represent them. All representatives are part of the U.N Agenda 21, toward the great reset to implement a new world in disorder. All parties use the deceptive ruse - Thesis, Antithesis, Synthesis to achieve the same objective while singing different tunes but the same lyric[25]. United Nations Agenda 21, the Rio Declaration on Environment and Development, and the Statement of principles for the Sustainable Management of Forests were adopted by more than 178 Governments at the United Nations Conference on Environment and Development (UNCED) held in Rio de Janeiro, Brazil, 3 to 14 June 1992[26]. Covid-19 meant to further the agenda of a totalitarian state.

---

[24] https://youtu.be/VlU8WAFixWs
[25] https://www.simplicityinthegospel.com/2018/12/deceptive-ruse-thesis-antithesis_20.html
[26] https://sustainabledevelopment.un.org/outcomedocuments/agenda21/

Its agenda is for total control of the entire world population. Control over all land, all water, all minerals, all plants, all animals, all construction, all food, all means of production, all energy, all information, and all human beings, which includes removing all your rights and freedoms, and including freedom of conscience, religion, culture, tradition, and behavior. It is about moving the population under city control. Their agenda is to drastically reduce the world population. The vaccine is used to achieve their murderous agenda to depopulate the earth population by 15% by 2050[27]. The vaccine is an experimental Gene therapy, a GMO generic modified organism, created to alter the DNA of people. This is a crime against humanity and should be act upon as such. Do your research. Do you understand that only a strong nationalist elected government can reverse their agenda.

What is coming soon?

The banking industry is coming together with the government to 'transform' Canadian society into the digital currency age preparing the way for the Mark of the Beast banking system, (Rev 13:17).

Derek Sloan, Leader of the Ontario Party warns us.
> "That this is our fight for freedom in the digital age, they (the government) tell you it will make your life easier, safer, and smarter. Don't fall for their misdirection. The medical industry, the

---

[27] https://thearcanelaboratory.com/watch-bill-gates-admits-to-human-depopulation-program/

banking industry, and Big Tech are coming together to push the implementation of a 'robust' digital ID. The Canadian Bankers Association has been promoting 'Why Canada needs a Digital Identity System' since at least 2018. Coupled with that, Interac, the financial system that controls all debit system transactions in Canada has also been publicly calling for a digital ID. They represent, and lobby on behalf of, over 60 banks and financial institutions in Canada, including the 'Big Five': CIBC, RBC, BMO, TD, and Scotia.

Now off the back of the pandemic, many other powerful organizations have joined together for an initiative called ID2020. These organizations include Mastercard, Facebook, The Rockefeller Foundation, IBM, and Microsoft. You guessed it… They are all calling on the government to create a digital ID. One of the convenient benefits they tote is a more **'streamlined process of vaccine attestation.'** Why are so many different powerful elements in society promoting what Hon. Justin Trudeau tells you it is just a digital driver's license? Because digital ID can transform how citizens interact with all goods and services in society. It can institutionalize compelled behaviour just as we saw with the Covid-19 shots." https://www.ontarioparty.ca

In Canada, most politicians, of all parties, including the Conservative Party of Canada except for The Ontario Party, and the Independence Party of Alberta use the skill of "Double Speak." It is too early to add that statement toward the United Conservative Party of Alberta. What is doublespeak? It is the skill as described by the North American Aboriginal who views the British colonial promises as speaking with a forked tongue. The American government used the same skill to deport thousands of Aboriginals to designated reserves, taking away all their ancestral land, customs, and traditions. That is to be expected under agenda 2021 and agenda 2030 in Canada, all citizens losing their identity as Canadian culture and traditions.

> *"Doublespeak is a language designed to evade responsibility. It makes the unpleasant appear pleasant, unattractive appear attractive. It is a language that pretends to communicate but really doesn't. It is a language designed to mislead while pretending not to. It is not a slip of the tongue or a mistake in the use of the language. It is done consciously and for a purpose[28]."*

Politicians use this skill of lying. Members of Parliament are not allowed to call each other liars in the House of Commons. The Bible is clear. Liars will not be part of the Kingdom of God, (Revelation 21:8). After all, their father is Satan the dragon, (Revelation 12:9)

Canada has no nationalist political parties at the federal level to represent the interest of the Canadian aspiration for economic sovereignty, security, and justice within a free democracy that will respect free speech and the right to be heard as written in the Canadian Bill of Rights.

---

[28] http://www.booknotes.org/Watch/10449-1/William-Lutz

Believers Are Salt of the Earth, A Light on a Lampstand

Before the pseudo-covid-19 pandemic, Canadian Christians were not persecuted, burned to the stake, crucified, stoned, beheaded, or forced to deny Christ and we are still not persecuted as such, since we comply with concessions. Canadian Christians were and are doormats, lukewarm, who have forgotten that they are to be a light on a lampstand and the salt of the earth. I am guilty as such also.

"Canadian ministries were the salt of the earth; but lost its flavour. Canadian ministries are then good for nothing but to be thrown out and trampled underfoot of the Liberal Party of Canada policies and as an example, by the LGBT2QI community," (Matt 5:13).

Salt and a light on a lampstand represent the truth. Believers of the truth are the Salt of the earth and Light on a lampstand, proclaiming God's word to be the truth. Canadian Christians are without excuses, who stop proclaiming the right to live according to the truth. Don't you know that your Christian faith, belief, moral values, and practices are protected by the Canadian Charter of Rights and Freedoms? Canadian institutions were founded on Judeo-Christian values. Canada has been built on the principles of Judeo-Christian faith and belief. Christians have the right to defend their lifestyle choices. To be a Christian or a 2SLGBTQIA+ is a behaviour choice, a lifestyle choice. That is called freedom of conscience. The 2SLGBTQIA+ community has no right to force their moral lifestyle on those who reject it. The government has no business in the bedroom. The Charter is for protecting all rights, not for imposing one sexual lifestyle preference on others.

Homosexual behaviour was viewed as a sin and a crime. Hon. Pierre Trudeau removed from the criminal code the crime of homosexuality stating that the government has no business in the bedroom. It was not long after this that the sin of homosexuality was accepted as a dysfunctional behaviour, but later as a lifestyle that required government legislation to protect it and to impose it on our children in all schools.

The Bible teaches Christians to show respect toward our government by recognizing and accepting that the governing powers are ordained by God. The Bible teaches us to pay our taxes and to pray for righteous leaders in government positions. It teaches us to live a quiet life and to do business with integrity. It teaches us to respect God's ordained marriage between one man and one woman. It teaches us to instruct and prepare our children for life's adult responsibilities. Yet so many do not have a spirit of discernment to view the government abuse and to oppose it.

Tell me, why would the government and the school board shy away from Christian values? Because it gives a notion that God is real and reminds the secular that one day all will give an account of their unbelief and their demeanour even the most defile and secret behaviour (Ecclesiastes 12:13–14).

It is a Christian's right to live by a set of beliefs. If a Christian wants to believe that Jesus was resurrected, which goes against all scientific evidence, it is his/her right to do so and The Charter of Rights and Freedoms supposedly will protect his/her belief. If a Christian wants to believe that the blue sky above is water as described in Genesis 1:6, which does not go against all scientific evidence, it is his/her right to do so and The Charter of Rights and Freedoms supposedly will protect his/her belief. The Charter of Rights and Freedoms has not been legislated to protect scientific evidence or unscientific speculation (pseudoscience) such as the theory of evolution or the big bang theory, but it has been enacted to protect the evidence of the written word of God. It is by faith that we understand.

What is wrong with teaching Christian values to our children? Is it not what sustains a healthy community? What is wrong with striving to love our neighbour as we love ourselves? To strive does not mean that we are perfect. For Christians, the good of the community is part of God's directives.

Christianity is not limited to the four walls of the Church Building

Bill of Rights

Marginal note: Recognition and declaration of rights and freedoms

It is hereby recognized and declared that in Canada there has existed and shall continue to exist without discrimination because of race, national origin, color, religion or sex, the following human rights, and fundamental freedoms, namely,

- the right of the individual to life, liberty, security of the person and enjoyment of property, and the right not to be deprived thereof except by due process of law.
- the right of the individual to equality before the law and the protection of the law.
- freedom of religion.
- freedom of speech.
- freedom of assembly and association; and
- freedom of the press.

The Charter of Rights and Freedoms will protect Equality Rights

- Every individual is equal before and under the law and has the right to equal protection and equal benefit of the law without discrimination and, in particular, without discrimination based on race, national or ethnic origin, colour, religion, sex, age or mental or physical disability.

Freedom of Worship vs. Freedom of Religion

Now, are we to shine our light within the four walls of the church building only? Nonsense. I have heard at the opening and closing prayers, pastors giving thanks to God for the freedom to worship, unaware that God has given them much more than a simple right to worship in Canada. It is God who wrote the constitution on His behalf - for His purpose, not ours.

Isn't it also for the United States of America with the Bill of Rights? He gave us, not the government, our freedom of religion. The Constitution was founded upon the principles that recognize the supremacy of God and the rule of law. Not any gods, but the Christian God – the God of Abraham, Isaac, and Jacob. The God who so loved the world that He gave His only begotten Son (Jesus), that whoever believes in Him should not perish but have everlasting life, (Jn 3:16).

What is the difference between freedom of worship and freedom of religion? The difference is that freedom of worship restricts a Christian's sphere of influence by living according to their beliefs, ethics, and moral standards and values within the walls of a building, while the freedom of religion gives Christians the freedom to carry their right to beliefs, ethics, and moral standard values everywhere in our society. It is our civil right. Have you not noticed how often we hear from the secular society to keep our religion at church? It is a constant attack on our rights.

Even Christians among themselves have demanded not to mix religion with politics... unthinkable. Too often I have been invited to a men's' fellowship breakfast or supper among Christian brothers and limited to small talk, avoiding talking about religion and politics. Apparently, it causes division. Is it not what the word of God supposed to do? We have become secular to the soul.

> *"For the word of God is living and powerful, and sharper than any two-edged sword, piercing even to the division of soul and spirit, and of joints and marrow, and is a discerner of the thoughts and intents of the heart,"* Hebrews 4:12

We have the fundamental right to peaceful assembly in a church environment and freedom of religion in a social environment, especially in our schools.

We are incapable of untangling ourselves from the snare unless we Christians, first repent and live by our personal faith, trusting in the Word.

Institutions, and the government will fail.

But God will never, never fail you.

> *"For it is impossible for those who were once enlightened, and have tasted the heavenly gift, and have become partakers of the Holy Spirit, and have tasted the good word of God and the powers of the age to come, if they fall away, to renew them again to repentance since they crucify again for themselves the Son of God and put Him to an open shame.*
>
> *For the earth which drinks in the rain that often comes upon it, and produces herbs useful for those by whom it is cultivated, receives blessings from God; but if it bears thorns and briers, it is rejected and near to being cursed,"* Hebrews 6:4-6

Christians are not the only citizens in this country which find themself tangle into the snare. Have we not been entrapped into the federal anti-multicultural policies - an autocratic snare, and anti-Christian snare, dictating what ought to be taught to our children, overruling the parent cultural and religious practice and belief, for the purpose to unite all cultures, all religious faith unto one philosophy, one ideology, one religion under the ruse of Interfaith indoctrination and Darwinism evolutionary rhetoric. We live in a so-called 'Extreme Bias Multiculturalism and in an Extreme Bias Multi-Gender' nation. Parent of all culture face the same dilemma, powerless.

> "True and pure diversity in a multicultural society is to allow each parent to teach their children their religious beliefs, their values

according to their culture and their tradition, and to teach their sexual moral standard and behaviour without prejudice and without interference from any level of government. Isn't that what The Charter of Rights and Freedoms represent?" (The author)

The Constitution of Canada does not belong to Parliament or to the Legislatures; it belongs to the people of this country, and it is there that the citizens of the country will find the protection of the rights to which they are entitled.

– *Nova Scotia (A.G.) v. Canada (A.G.) [1951] S.C.R. 31*

After all, the Constitution is a document for the people and one of the most important goals of any system of dispute resolution is to serve well those who make use of it.

– *Reference Re Residential Tenancies Act [1996] 1 S.C.R. 186, @ p. 210*

The Church of the Laodiceans
The Greatest Revival

There are many church pastors who are praying and hoping for a revival. Some for a spiritual restoration of the true gospel, for some, preparing for the return of Jesus (the rapture) and some hoping that it will bring about a restoration of the sovereignty of this nation. Pastors, your heart reflects the heart of Nehemiah. Nehemiah represents God's people who desire God to continue to bless the reconstruction of Jerusalem's wall and the Temple, (Nehemiah 5:19, 13:14,22,31).

> *"Remember me, my God, for good, according to all that I have done for this people,"* Nehemiah 5:19.
>
> *"Remember me, O my God, concerning this, and do not wipe out my good deeds that I have done for the house of my God, and for its services,"* Nehemiah 13:14!

Ministers, pastors, and teachers who are God's stewards, the example of Nehemiah is for you. You love God and want dearly to serve Him. You want to do more. I can assure you that God has not forgotten you. In due time He will answer your prayers.

In the United States, there is a revival, a return to God's word, a return to God's values hoping for a restoration of a sovereign nation. As of now, in Canada, there is no sign of a spiritual revival. There is no increase in attendance in churches nationwide. Unfortunately, quite the opposite, more and more churches are closing.

It could be that since the Covid-19 lockdown many members prefer the cozy comfort of their home to follow their pastor on Web broadcast or follow pastors of other teaching preference. Teaching about end-time prophecies substantially has increased the interest of many Canadians. But a change of heart, recognizing the nation's sins, an increased interest in God's word, a spirit of repentance, and a desire to change have not come about. Most of the population recognizes the corruption and abuse of our government authority but do not recognize the hand of God in choosing leaders that reflects the state of their heart.

> *"Let every soul be subject to the governing authorities. For there is no authority except from God, and the authorities that exist are appointed by God,"* Romans 13:1

Canadians Rejected God
Christians Rejected Knowledge, the Truth

It all started when Lucifer rejected God with one-third of the angels who rebelled against God. God planned to create a special people that He could call His own made thru faith (a decision to trust and obey God). He created an environment as a training ground, created the heavens and earth. Then, man and woman were created in God's image, and He gave dominion over the whole earth. Satan rages with envy and applied a ruse to derail God's intent. Using the skill of "Double Speak," he deceived Eve, followed by Adam.

From then on, the truth was in constant attack. There are few details about the pre-flood period, except through the Book of Enoch. What we know is that there was no government, no law, and therefore, no institution to enforce the law, order, and justice. Everybody was behaving according to their own heart. It was total depravity. Even falling angels got involved to manipulate the DNA of God's creation.

Yet, there was an attempt at a revival through the ministry of Enoch. Whatever took Enoch to repent (a turn within the heart) and to walk with God for 300 years, it is not told. His first sixty-five years were about learning to walk with God, I guess. Was it by faith (believing and trusting God)? It is not told. If it were important, the Holy Spirit would have told us. The trend throughout the Bible is that righteousness was attained by faith alone, an act of grace on the part of God, (2 Peter 2:4-21).

The book of Enoch is not in the Canon. Not surprising since the Romanists did everything for the truth not to be accessible. Yet, we know that many books were written, such as the Book of Enoch, Slavonic Enoch, the Book of Jubilees, and the Book of Moses, (Eccl 12:12). Enoch ministered to angels, and man/woman. Fallen angels are eternally condemned, without access to salvation (2 Peter 2:4). In the pre-flood era, there is no mention of idol worshiping and adultery. Mankind has proven that it has a sinful nature, total depravity, and uncontrolled by far indescribable, all according to their heart,

> *"But as the days of Noah were, so also will the coming of the Son of Man be,"*
> Matthew 24:37.

The pre-flood citizens have rejected God and His truth; therefore, Enoch's revival failed.

Sixty-nine years after Enoch's rapture to heaven, a man was born and was found righteous, Noah. Was it through Enoch's ministry that he heard of the truth and was found righteous? It is not told. Was it by one seed of truth thru Methuselah and Lamech? We are not told. Can we assume that Enoch's revival succeeds in planting a seed? There is no mention if Methuselah and Lamech were found righteous either. It is my view that there are books that are purposely hidden. Noah ministered for 120 years, and Enoch for 300 years, both stood out as a light in a corrupted civilization that rejected the truth, refusing to repent and to be saved.

After the flood, it was a new beginning, the fear of God's wrath and grace was constantly revealed to mankind. The rainbow appearance was its reminder. Yet mankind again became again defiant. The building of a tower was a sign of defiance. God did not plan for a revival of the truth; the tower of babel was proof that they rejected God's truth and authority. God causes confusion by creating new languages, which forces them to disperse worldwide. That is why Babel is known through traditions to be the origin of all religions, a sign of defiance against God's truth.

God's plan for a revival of the truth was to be witnessed throughout all the earth. Through a special people called His own. It all started with one man, Abram, later known as

Abraham. The purpose of the nation of Israel was to reflect God's righteousness and truth to all surrounding nations. Yet they failed. God constantly sent prophets in an attempt for a revival in Israel, then in Judah. Success and failure were their legacies. The greatest attempt for a revival was through Jesus Christ, Son of God, and the awaited Messiah whom they rejected. God's judgment and wrath resulted in the fall of Jerusalem, the destruction of the Temple and the dispersion of the Jews worldwide leaving the nation in total desolation.

Yet, Jesus' revival was not a total failure. A few thousand Jews followed by Gentiles accepted with immense joy the message of truth, first through the testimony of His disciples and then by a multitude of believers from all over the known world. Jesus' revival spread like a wildfire, there was no stopping it. This is the new era of a revival that will last until Jesus returns, (Matthew 16:18). Darkness shall not prevail against the Church. From the church's early beginning till our modern time, the good news has reached all corners of the world.

What defines a revival? What defines a successful revival? According to the dictionary, "a revival is a restoration to use, acceptance, activity, or vigour after a period of obscurity or quiescence. From a church perspective, it is a concentrated work of God where Christians in various churches earnestly desire more of Christ, boldness in witness, and commitment to missions."

Isn't what the church was commissioned to be and to do from the beginning? The church's mission is to be the salt of the earth, which means a preservative of the truth. The church is also commanded to be a light on the lampstand, which is to be present in all areas of our society even in its darkest hour. Take the example of Lot, he successfully ministered a revival, and God counted him as righteous,

> *"he was oppressed by the filthy conduct of the wicked (for that righteous man, dwelling among them, tormented his righteous soul from day to day by seeing and hearing their lawless deeds),"* (2 Peter 2:7-8).

Lot was sitting at the gate of Sodom, (Genesis 19:1). Tradition says that he was a member of the city council, actively involved in resolving disputes among the citizens of Sodom. He was a light in a sinful dark environment. He was viewed as righteous by God since Lot actively took part in a revival. I conclude that a successful revival is not measured by the number of people saved or who respond actively by repenting and returning to the truth, but mainly by the action of one individual who represents God's truth.

How many among you are the only believer in the truth in your family? How many among you are the only believer at work, the office, or at a construction site? Your presence reflects God's principalities, isn't it? Your moral values are constantly being challenged to ridicule. The existence of a righteous God, the creator is always questioned, "How can a just God order the killing of an entire tribe, women and children, in the Old Testament?" You are a lot like Lot. You are part of a revival in your way by being in obedience to God. Didn't the first believers of Christ's resurrection call the Way by Paul, (Acts 9:2)?

Many are calling for a revival for the purpose of turning a nation around to its previous socially wealthy economy and freedom condition. Is that the real purpose? Is it the economic wealth of our nation of the past few decades that causes the modern church to be like the Laodiceans church or is it our nation sin condition, a turn away from God?

> *"Because you say, 'I am rich, have become wealthy, and have need of nothing, (do not need God)"* (Rev 3:17).

Many want an increase in attendance at the assembly of the church? Many view our time as signs of Jesus' imminent return and therefore, do not want to bother to be part of a revival. Many accept the status quo and view no hope in a revival since the elites are winning the game as prophesied. And many believe that it is business as usual, nothing to see here since all things are okeydokey. All have missed the point, and that included me at one time. When I started to write in my blog years ago, it was for the purpose of sharing what I needed to learn, and learn I have.

A revival comes with great responsibilities. One of the responsibilities is to be in obedience to God. Take the example of King Saul. He was to take part in a great revival, consisting of cleansing the land from the Amalekites (1 Sam 15). Utterly destroying all that they had, not to spare them. Both man and woman, infant and nursing child, ox and sheep, camel, and donkey. Saul failed. He spared Agag the king and the best of the livestock, keeping it for a sacrifice to the Lord. King Saul failed as Cain failed.

> *"Has the Lord as great delight in burnt offerings and sacrifices, as in obeying the voice of the Lord? Behold, to obey is better than sacrifice, and to heed than the fat of rams,"* (1 Samuel 15:22).

What is the spirit of Cain? It is 'not taking Jesus by His word.' In (James 1:22), we read; *"But be doers of the word and not hearers only, deceiving yourselves."* I invite you to read my commentary titled, "The Spirit of Cain"[29]. If you fail to understand why God acts so differently in the New

---

[29] https://www.simplicityinthegospel.com/2012/08/spirit-of-cain.html

Testament than in the Old Testament, please study the subject of "Dispensation[30]."

There always has been a revival, it is just that people have not been listening.

There are no signs of a revival without the truth being revealed.

> "There is no revival without obedience from those to whom the truth has been revealed and given the responsibility to share it."

The Rise of the Romanists

Many Christians spared their lives by leaving Jerusalem. Obeying Jesus' warning that when they would see Jerusalem surrounded by armies, then they should flee from the city (Luke 21:20-21). They escaped persecution, but it was only for a brief time. Since they accepted Jesus as Lord alone and did not genuflect to Caesar as a god it brought great persecution within the first few centuries. The suffering which they endured brought Christians nearer to one another and to their Redeemer. Their living example and dying testimony were constant witnesses to the truth. Since the torture and death through lions feasting on them or crucifixion failed to interrupt the spreading of the gospel, Satan's strategy changed to infiltrating the Church. Under the guise of a godly bishop, he proposed that Christians should make concessions that all might unite on the platform of belief in Christ only, without the conviction of sin, no need for repentance, and therefore, no change of heart. Many yielded and modified some features of their faith, uniting with those

---

[30] https://youtu.be/VnTj--yWydY

who had accepted a part of Christianity. It became a cloak of faked Christianity. Satan took a foothold in the church, to corrupt its faith and to turn minds from the word of truth. The seed of tares has been sown in the field of wheat. It will be as such until the end of time before Jesus' return for the harvest. I invite you to read my article titled, "INTERFAITH - The Gathering Of The Tares". [31]

As the followers of Christ have united with idolaters, the Christian religion has become corrupt, and the church has lost its purity and power. Satan pats himself on the back, he didn't believe that it would be so easy. Once the majority of the deceived followers were reached, he took more authority over them and inspired them to persecute those who remain true to God. Freedom of conscience to accept the simplicity of the gospel was replaced with the doctrine of Lordship Salvation and were coerced into complete obedience to the Pope and Christ's authority on earth, with the threat of being excommunicated. As it is today, to preserve peace and freedom many have decided to compromise with false theologies, false doctrines, and fatal delusions. Many are now regarded with favor by thousands who claim to be followers of Christ. Just stating that you believe in Jesus alone doesn't make you a Christian. The true gospel is a gospel of reconciliation with the living God, the Creator, Who desires that no one perishes. His grace and mercy are so great and abundant that reconciliation was made easy. His Son Jesus Christ did all the work on the cross to reconcile us to Him. The work is defined as His death, His burial, and His resurrection. By grace alone through faith alone in Jesus alone. Yes, repentance is required, which is to recognize our sinful nature and

---

[31] https://www.simplicityinthegospel.com/2013/05/interfaith-gathering-of-tares.html

that only through Christ can anyone be transformed. I invite you to read my commentary titled, "Repentance is a must."[32]

Compromise... the era of compromise.

Many Canadians including I have made compromises. If not so, why are there so many different denominations? All churches have their personalized Statement of Belief. In 2011, I wrote a commentary titled, "Christianity is like the menu of an Ice Cream Parlour".[33] I once attended a men's fellowship breakfast. One point of interest that I enjoyed was hearing the testimony of my brothers in Christ, and how they got saved. So, I went around the table and asked if they would share the moment and the circumstance where they accepted Jesus as Lord. Many were excited to share with gladness, yet some were offended that I asked. What does that tell you? More likely this individual is not saved. The reality is that the truth has been watered down and compromised, to meaningless tradition. I came from Romanist culture and tradition, full of conditions for salvation by works with no true repentance, except through the constant fear and reminder of hell. Nowadays the Bible is viewed as a fairy tale, God is good, where there is no hell, and everybody goes to heaven. Many believe that they can talk to their lost loved ones in heaven.

I invite you to read my commentary titled, "Praying to Dead Saints or loved ones[34]". The common narrative is that you

---

[32] https://www.simplicityinthegospel.com/2011/07/repentance-is-must.html
[33] https://www.simplicityinthegospel.com/2011/01/christianity-is-like-menu-of-ice-cream.html

[34] https://www.simplicityinthegospel.com/2009/11/praying-to-dead-saints-or-love-one.html

do not need Jesus as an intermediary between you and God, that their lost one intercedes for them.

The Romanist agenda is the same as today and that is to keep the population dumb, keep them away from the truth and make a financial gain. Keeping the Bible out of reach and in Latin only accessible to scholars and intellectuals who submit to the pope's authority. Any defying the Romanist doctrine were accused of heresy and threatened with excommunication. That was important. Once excommunicated you were shunned by society. It became difficult to do business, to trade, sell and buy. Your silence was required if not, torture, imprisonment, to be burned at the stake were the consequences. Is there anything new under the sun?

The globalists in collusion with the papacy use the same tactic of fear against the world population. Covid-19 is used to bring the population to submission. A constant false narrative of extreme danger from the virus, and extreme measures used through mandates, coerce tactics to be vaccinated or else lose your job and be shunned by society. And if speaking out against the government covid-19 mandate such as Randy Hillier[35], who served as a member of provincial parliament (MPP) in the Legislative Assembly of Ontario from 2007-2022. Hillier represented the riding of Lanark—Frontenac—Kingston as an independent MPP from 2019 to 2022. He was removed from the PC Party by Premier Doug Ford in 2019 for being outspoken against the use of facemasks, vaccines, and lockdowns during the COVID-19 pandemic. He spent extensive time at the "Freedom Convoy".

Former MP Conservative Party Derek Sloan travelled across Ontario to speak at protests and demonstrations against public health measures enacted in response to the COVID-19

---

[35] https://www.randyhilliermpp.com/about

pandemic. On April 24, 2021, Sloan spoke at an anti-lockdown protest in Barrie where he recommended that the government explore treating COVID-19 using Vitamin D. The following day Sloan, Ontario MPP Randy Hillier, and other demonstrators attended a service at the Church of God in Aylmer in defiance of the Reopening Ontario Act, which limits in-person religious gatherings to ten people. Sloan has also attended demonstrations in Ottawa, Peterborough, Stratford, and Chatham. Sloan was charged in relation to the event in Aylmer and has been investigated by Belleville police regarding a gathering at Zwicks Park. Dereck Sloan is now leader of the Ontario Party[36]

There was massive protest in cities across Canada by concern educated Canadians, doctors and pastors who protests against public health measures, against the controversial vaccine mandate including the unjustified vaccine passport and were fined or incarcerated. Their names have been mentioned in this book.

The Romanist influence on our modern society has pushed the truth further and further away from a loving Father in heaven. The magic of technology, the miracle of modern medicine, and the creativity of the human mind led to the imagination of the origin of an endless universe without God as the Creator, in an unproven theory of the Big Bang, and the theory of evolution. All very profitable lies.

> *"The Lord is not slack concerning His promise, as some count slackness, but is longsuffering toward us, not willing that any should perish but that all should come to repentance,"* 2 Peter 3:9

---

[36] https://www.ontarioparty.ca/

Our modern western churches would not be able to go through the persecution that our ancestors went through, (John 15:20). Only a few did, such as Pastor Artur Pawlowski, Pastor Tobias Tissen, Pastor Tim Stephens, Pastor Henry Hildebrandt and assistant Pastor Peter Wall and Pastor James Coates. Then there is the extraordinary dedication from Pastor Steven Michel of Crosspoint Baptist Church in Navan, Ontario, Canada who took action to serve his members by delivering 14/1hrs services from Saturday to Sunday when there was a restriction of ten attendees per church service. That is devotion.

I am aware that there are more heroes that need to be mention. I am sorry that I didn't get to known you. I thank you for your involvement in fighting the fight for our freedoms and our rights.

We are disturbed and dismayed to see our rights and freedoms denied for the sake of a virus no more dangerous than the flu virus. One week into the lockdown, I recognized that it was a fraud, a ruse to control the population. It is called the gift of discernment. And now we know that it was all orchestrated. The Covid Lies[37] - Doctor Mike Yeadon's document

> *"And this I pray, that your love may abound still more and more in knowledge and **all** discernment,"* Philippians 1:9

Have you notice that I underline and bold the word ***all***?

I am a student of Bible prophecy. Study God's word and He reveal all thing to you.

---

[37] https://rumble.com/embed/v113v4n/?pub=gi6jj

> *"Surely the Lord God does nothing,*
>
> *Unless He reveals His secret to His servants the prophets,"* Amos 3:7
>
> *"No longer do I call you servants, for a servant does not know what his master is doing; but I have called you friends, for all things that I heard from My Father I have made known to you,"* John 15:15

I am not perfect in my walk with the Lord, so therefore, what wound make me different who have not a medical degree to come to a quick conclusion that the Covid-19 pandemic was staged and a fraud? In my daily prayer I would say the following, "Deliver us from evil, the lies and the deceptions."

It did not take long that I was right. People were not falling ill in substantial numbers in my neighborhood, the hospital were not busy with covid-19 cases as reported by the mainstream media. There were many nurses who did not comply with the covid-19 emergency policies such as Kristen Nagle of London, Kristal Pitter of Tillsonburg and Sara Choujounian of Toronto who have been investigated by the College of Nurses of Ontario (CNO) for sharing their controversial views about the pandemic on social media[38].

As time progresses, video on the controversial pandemic emergency policies has also been exposed by expert on social media such as Doctor Andrew Kaufman who read the first virology papers out of Wuhan in December 2019, he was shocked to discover that the scientists had come nowhere close to proving that a new virus had emerged… yet

---

[38] https://www.cbc.ca/news/canada/london/ontario-nurses-pandemic-libel-suit-1.6307238

saw the media and authorities already claiming a viral pandemic was on it's way[39].

Unfortunately, people were gripped by the mainstream media and by the time they awake they realize that the pandemic was a fraud and they also realized that we have lost our sovereignty and our freedoms.

God gave us a Charter of Rights and Freedoms and we didn't use it to protect our children. Only a few past victories from courageous parents with no financial support to pay for their lawyer's fee. As an example, a stand-alone young couple challenged the Hamilton Children's Aid Society for removing two young girls from their foster home because they refused, based upon their Christian beliefs, to stipulate that the Easter Bunny and Santa were real. They used The Charter of Rights and Freedoms in the Ontario Superior Court of Justice. In his concluding statement, Justice Goodman recognized that freedoms of religion, as understood in Canada, allows individuals to embrace, openly declare, and manifest their beliefs.

Citizens are free to live their lives in conformity with their beliefs, and that the state, on the other hand, is to be neutral on matters of religion. Why is it then that this verdict is not used to disallow the school board to indoctrinate of perverted lifestyle to our Christian children? You can read the details and review the court case on the Canadian Council of Christian Charities website, article title, "Lie, or Lose Your Children"[40]

---

[39] https://rumble.com/vy9mv7-the-viral-delusion-part-1-behind-the-curtain-of-the-plandemic-and-the-pseud.html

[40] https://www.cccc.org/news_blogs/intersection/2018/04/04/lie-or-lose-your-children/

Face it, we have lost the salt flavour. It seems as if God has taken away the light with the lampstand. The fact is that we Christians cover up the light. Please read my article title, "Christians - The Guardian of The Charter of Rights and Freedoms."[41]

Whether through reform or a revival... the truth, God's word must expose the lies, (Ephesians 5:11)

There always has been a revival, in all eras of spiritual darkness through centuries past. Here are a few who made a historical impact that has continued into our modern time; The Waldenses, John Wycliffe, Huss and Jerome, the Bohemia reformers, Martin Luther, the Swiss reformer, the reform in Germany, the French revolution reformers, the Netherlands and Scandinavian reformers, English reformers, the Pilgrim Father reformers, the American reformers, and many modern revivalists.

You could read about all their legacies in a book titled, "The Great Controversy," by E.G White, ISBN 978-1-629131-72-6.

All the reformers were part of a great revival through the centuries. They are the authors of the American Bill of Rights and the Canadian Charter of Rights and Freedoms.

There were many revivals by unknown stewards of God, even though they perished, they left their imprint of faith over all who witnessed their act of courage in obedience to God. You might not know their names. They were Chinese, North Korean, Iranian, Saudi Arabian, and from many other nations where Christianity is forbidden.

---

[41] https://www.simplicityinthegospel.com/2019/11/christians-stand-on-guard-for-thee.html

What about us, the Canadian? The most lukewarm church in the whole western nation? President Joe Bidden declares that "Our Darkest Days Are Ahead of Us." Is it a warning to the churches? Are you frightened by the present social economic condition? How should you view reports from the media? Should we be alarmed? Shouldn't we view it from God's perspective?

"God does not forget or neglect His children but permits the wicked to reveal their true character, that none who desire to do His will may be deceived concerning them. Again, the righteous are placed in the furnace of affliction, that they themselves may be purified: that their example may convince others of the reality of faith and godliness; and also, that their consistent course may condemn the ungodly and unbelieving. God permits the wicked to prosper and to reveal their enmity against Him, that when they shall have filled up the measure of their iniquity all may see His justice and mercy in their utter destruction." page 21 of "The Great Controversy."

> *"I am the light of the world. He who follows Me shall not walk in darkness but have the light of life."* John 8:12

> *"Rest in the Lord, and wait patiently for Him; Do not fret because of him who prospers in his way, Because of the man who brings wicked schemes to pass,"* Psalm 37:7

When I accepted Christ, I dreaded being persecuted for my beliefs. I believed living as a Christian would be easy in Canada. After all, I was a Catholic for the first part of my life. I was sure that starting to attend a protestant church would make no difference. I was wrong. I might have not been burned of the stake, but I was threatened excommunication. I was treated differently from my siblings; they were embarrassed to be around me when I professed my love for Jesus.

I attended a church which assembled on the Sabbath. The Sabbath starts at sunset Friday to sunset Saturday. I kept the Jewish feast days and abstained from eating unclean meat and unclean fish. Now, it was extremely hard to conceal my faith compared to traditional secular Christianity. People in my workplace were distant. I did not like to be different; these doctrines were given too much attention. But here I was living as a Messianic Jew. To read more about my journey to salvation, please read my testimony titled, "When Did I Receive The Gift of Eternal Life?"[42]

Back to the subject of a revival. I concluded that it never did stop. Revival encountered opposition when the church let its guard down as described by the letter to the church of the Laodiceans.

> *"I know your works, that you are neither cold nor hot. I could wish you were cold or hot. So then, because you are lukewarm, and neither cold nor hot, I will vomit you out of my mouth. Because you say, 'I am rich, have become wealthy, and have need of nothing'—and do not know that you are wretched, miserable, poor, blind, and naked,"* Revelation 3:15 17

---

[42] https://www.simplicityinthegospel.com/2013/10/when-did-i-receive-gift-of-eternal-life.html

Is this how our churches actually look in the eyes of God?

Wow... does this describe the North American church of the 21st century? We do not see how vulnerable we are by putting all our trust in man's institutions. Wealthy, rich in need of nothing but spiritually blind, content with once-a-week assembly, no personal time with God, no spiritual character development, no sharing of the gospel, no involvement in politics, whether on school boards, municipal councils, provincial and federal politics. We became enchanted by the magic of technology and the security of conscience trusting our politicians. One by one our values were taken away, even our sovereign right to be the sole parent of our children. Folks, wake up, the government owns the children through their birth certificates. It is hard to identify a Christian in our modern society. Thank God that He offers a way out of our complacency.

> *"Therefore, be zealous and repent. Behold, I stand at the door and knock. If anyone hears My voice and opens the door, I will come into him and dine with him, and he with Me,"* Revelation 3:19-20. *"As many as*

I love, I rebuke and chasten." "...buy from Me gold refined in the fire" v.18.

Go back to God's words that have been proven to be true. *"...anoint your eyes with eye salve,"* an ointment to take away your blindness. How do I get that? By praying for a spirit of discernment. What happens to us when we neglect to study God's word (*dine with him, and he with Me*), with personal and weekly Bible study among brothers in Christ? Our souls become isolated just the nation of Israel became. In what way did the church become desolated? God causes a great spiritual famine. Since His words were not actively used, He allows ungodly man to indoctrinate our children.

> *"He deprives the trusted ones of speech And takes away the discernment of the elders,"* (Job 12:20).

Jesus is talking to you and me here. He will take the lampstand and the light away from this country and will give it to someone else. Right now, the one that deserves the most of God's light are the Chinese, the Korean, and the Kenyan Christians, anybody else but Canadians.

> *"Yes, if you cry out for discernment,*
> *And lift up your voice for understanding,*
> *If you seek her as silver,*
> *And search for her as for hidden treasures;*
> *Then you will understand the fear of the Lord,*
> *And find the knowledge of God,"*
> Proverbs 2:3-5

The answers my friend for a revival in this nation lie within the Canadian heart. Do you have the desire for the word of God? Do you have the love for His truth?

Are you being cherry pickers, choosing what is appealing only, better known as itching ears, (2 Timothy 4:3-4). We live in an ocean of lies way over our heads, and we have forgotten how to walk on water, by faith, in trusting in Jesus. For so many, they learn to swim, that is trying to make faith work rather than letting faith do the work.

> *"And this I pray, that your love may abound still more and more in knowledge and **all discernment**, that you may approve the things that are excellent, that you may be sincere and without offence till the day of Christ, being filled with <u>the fruits of righteousness which are by Jesus Christ</u>, to the glory and praise of God,"* Phil 1:9-11

Is anyone able to walk on water in the Lord perfectly and without complaint? We are human beings after all. We are not robots. We have a free will and the freedom of conscience. It is a gift of God. Satan will do anything to take it away. The only time that your will and freedom of conscience will be in Satan's hand is when you accept the mark of the beast as described in Revelation 14. There will be no turning back, (Revelation 14:9-11)

The Bible tells us that *"For by grace you have been saved through faith, and that not of yourselves; it is the gift of God, not of works, lest anyone should boast,* (Eph 2:8-9).

"To be sincere and without offense till the day of Christ, being filled with the fruits of righteousness which are by Jesus Christ, to the glory and praise of God," does this describe the characteristics of all God's reformists during the past century who challenged the Romanists?

What is to be sincere and without offence? Is it to be fearless, and shameless to be called steward of God, (Romans 10:11)? We are all called for a purpose, in a position to labour for Christ. Whatever condition and circumstance God call you in our time is to witness His grace and mercy among all men. We might have a special office in the church, (1 Corinthians

12:28) but the bottom line is to witness the glory of God of what He has done for you. You do not need to be a scholar to confess that Jesus is Lord and that you believe with all your heart that Jesus has resurrected.

The religions of this world have the same social attribute, which is to love our neighbour and help those in the need. They reflect God's characteristic to love toward all men, women, and children but without Jesus in the picture. We are created in His image.

> *"Pure and undefiled religion before God and the Father is this: to visit orphans and widows in their trouble and to keep oneself unspotted from the world,"* James 1:27.

The key role and purpose of the church is to be salt and a light on a lampstand. Continuing in the truth. Once God opens your eyes to His truth, you should share it. That is the reason I write what I have learned. Share it with your brothers in Christ and discuss it. You do not need to be at a pulpit in front of an assembly. If you come across a stranger, be prepared to answer his questions. No need to be intellectual. Only a seed is required; God will water it. Keep it simple. Remember, they have already heard it all and seen it all from the perspective of tele-evangelists, so many have been turned off. When someone asks why your gospel is different from others explain that Jesus said, *"For many will come in My name, saying, 'I am the Christ,' and will deceive many,"* Matthew 24:5.

What else can we do? We need to pray for those who suffered from the result of the Covid lockdown, for those who suffer the serious side effects of the vaccine which are irreversible and for those who lost a loved one due to vaccination. There has been report of an increase suicide among the teenagers, yet there is no document found in the government archives. The last report was dated in 2018.

The unknown causes of death[43] are on the rise, and it will get even worse among the vaccinated.

Alberta, Canada: Unprecedented Rise in Deaths from 'Unknown Causes' Becomes Leading Killer in 2020 and 2021[44]

'Unknown Cause' Is the Top Cause of Death in Canada![45]

The blame will be on those who did not receive the jab. Jezebel way of setting up false accusations which is still exceedingly popular among the modern-day Romanists, (1 Kings 21:8). The self-proclaimed elite have created a new cult, a new religion with the same coercion tactic as it was in the days of the reformist, 'Vaccinology' the belief that vaccination will cure all illnesses. As it was in the days of the corrupted Romanists who profit from indulgences for salvation, so do the modern Romanist (Luciferians) profit from the lies of vaccination. If you deviate from their belief, from that cult, you are shunned by society. Doctors, practitioners, and nurses lose their right to practice. If you are an employee, you are put on a leave of absence, losing the right to sustain your family. If you are a self-entrepreneur, you lose your customers. There is extraordinarily strong propaganda claiming that the unvaccinated are the cause of spreading this imaginary virus which is no more dangerous than the flu. It all lies. It started by putting all our trust in the magic of science and the miracle of medication. Is there corruption in all levels of government, the medical establishment, and professionals?

Have you heard of the new Canadian's cure for depression

---

[43] https://rumble.com/embed/v1bl5br/
[44] https://adversereactionreport.com/reactions/alberta-canada-unprecedented-rise-in-deaths-from-unknown-causes-becomes-leading-killer-in-2020-and-2021/
[45] https://www.globalresearch.ca/unknown-cause-top-cause-death-canada/5791610

"Trudeau's MAID Euthanasia Program To Allow Doctors To Kill Kids Without Parental Consent - Kid depress because he doesn't have a girlfriend," Tucker Carlson Tonight[46]

"Canada uses doctors to kill the weakest in the nation, whether the homeless, a depressed elderly because no one visits her/him, and now a suicidal teenager," Tucker Carlson Tonight.

> *"And I will come near you for judgment; I will be a swift witness Against sorcerers, Against adulterers, Against perjurers, Against those who exploit wage earners and widows and orphans, And against those who turn away an alien— Because they do not fear Me," Says the Lord of hosts,"* Malachi 3:5

Satan never stops, covering up the truth by deceiving. In Canada and U.S.A. medicine is for a profit industry, according to a whistle-blower, he continues in his statement that the population bow to the Alter of MD direct high-tech medicine at the population demise. Doctors taking advantage of the sick patients is not new, it happens when Jesus was among men.

> *"Now a woman, having a flow of blood for twelve years, who had spent all her livelihood on physicians and could not be healed by any,"* Luke 8:43

Thanks God that there are still many honest doctors with integrity.

---

[46] https://youtu.be/nX4MURUeLog

Satan's power is all in his tongue. Satan is beautiful, (2 Cor 11:14) and intelligent, (Ez 28:17), crafty, (Gen 3:1) but small and weak in appearance, (Isaiah 14:16-17), so weak that only one angel subdues and shackles him (Rev 20:1-2). Satan is in command, the high commander over his angels constantly at war against God's children and His angels, (Rev 12:7-9). Satan is not omnipresent. He can only be present in one place at a time. He has a legion of angels, and demons to fulfill his malicious mischief. His throne is always at the greatest center of culture and commerce as it was once Ancient Pergamos. Prophecy foretold that Babylon would resurrect once more as the greatest center of commerce, (Rev 18:10-11).

Lucifer uses a technique called Pseudoscience to deceive. Pseudoscience is a claim, belief, or practice, which is falsely presented as scientific facts, but does not adhere to a valid scientific method, cannot be reliably tested, or otherwise lacks scientific status. Hoax science is a better name for this kind of science.

Satan's purpose is to hide God, proclaiming that you do not have a Father. Biblically speaking, those who teach pseudoscience are called false teachers and false prophets, magicians, astrologers, sorcerers, and soothsayers.

Satan has also men and women who choose to follow him. They willingly serve him or serve him by deceit.

> *"They are darkened in their understanding and separated from the life of God because of the ignorance that is in them due to the hardening of their hearts,"* (Eph 4:18).

They are accomplices, and responsible for mass murder, believing that they will not be accountable for crime against humanity. If only they would heed to God's grace.

The Rapture
Until then, keep busy sharing the gospel as if it will be 50 years from now

> *"Then He* (Jesus) *said to His disciples, "The harvest truly is plentiful, but the laborers are few. Therefore pray the Lord of the harvest to send out laborers into His harvest,"* Matthew 9:37-38

There always has been a revival. Isn't the church prevailing, (Matthew 16:18)? As much as God upheld His promises to keep David's descendants alive until the Messiah established His reign on earth, God is keeping His promise to keep His Church alive until Christ returns. There was a time in history when labourers were few. There were many reasons why there were few labourers in some eras, persecution was the reason.

Yet, through persecution the response has been increasing personal testimony of the gospel, the truth proves to be more powerful than the opposing forces.

> *"And God has appointed these in the church: first apostles, <u>second prophets</u>, <u>third teachers</u>, after that miracle, then gifts of healings, helps, administrations, varieties of tongues,"* 1 Corinthians 12:28

Many of these appointees' functions are presently active in the Church. The office of Apostle was God's hand-picked chosen by Jesus preparing the proclamation of the kingdom to the Jews first. Then to Gentiles making disciples as ministers in the church. The Apostles completed the writing of the New Testament Scriptures. It is to be given to teachers as servants of God, (2 Peter 1:19, Romans 12:1-5). Since the word of God is completely revealed in the scriptures, nothing else needs to be added for interpretation, therefore the office of Apostles has been drawn to an end.

> *"And so we have the prophetic word confirmed, which you do well to heed as a light that shines in a dark place until the day dawns and the morning star rises in your hearts; knowing this first, that no prophecy of Scripture is of any private interpretation,"* 2 Peter 1:19-20.

In our era of lukewarm churches, the subject of the imminent return of Jesus, the rapture is a hot topic for students of Bible prophecy. There are books, eBooks, radio broadcasts, TV, movies and internet platforms from scholars, and even self-proclaimed prophets. Some are audacious and predict Jesus return right to the day and hour. Interpretation of end-time prophecy has become very profitable. So many who face life challenges are looking forward to the rapture. It is our blessed hope, the promise of Jesus's return to take away the Church before the terrible and dreadful period called the great tribulation.

There are teachers of eschatology with many difference opinions about when the rapture event will take place. Some are pre-tribulation, some mid-tribulation, some pos-tribulation, and some do not believe in the rapture but a final resurrection of the dead for the final judgment. There is a constant accusation of heresy among Christians who have different opinions. Let us make it clear, it is not in believing the time of Christ's return that saves us from the fire of hell, but rather declaring that Jesus is Lord, believing in His resurrection, the proof that His mission has been accomplished, "it is finished," (Romans 10:9, John 19:30).

If all of God's stewards from past centuries would have waited in idly for the rapture, there would not have been any reform and any revival. There would have been no Waldenses, no John Wycliffe, no Huss and no Jerome, no Bohemia reformers, and no Martin Luther revivals.

How would the Church prevail without God sending special stewards who answered the call of duty as He had called Enoch, Noah, Moses, and many prophets and many stewards such as Ezra who prepared his heart to seek the law of the Lord, and to do it, and to teach statutes and ordinances in Israel, (Ezra 7:10)?

Have you noticed a pattern? Have you noticed that God chose and prepared someone special for a special time? There always has been a time when humanity went into a period of darkness, an absence of God's truth. Aren't we living in such a time now when the word of God has sunk in an ocean of lies?

Until then, *"work; for I am with you,"* said the Lord to Zerubbabel and to Joshua. That applies to us also. (Haggai 2:4).

DO YOU GET THE POINT?

Will the church of Laodicea, especially the Western Churches be part of the greatest revival, the greatest reform of all centuries? It has already started. There are so many stewards right now who are reaching out, focusing on preaching the simplicity of the gospel. There are outreach programs on the internet on various platforms. Stop arguing about who has the right formula for salvation. It is simple. We are saved by Jesus, by His words, by His blood, by faith in believing in all the above which is by an act of grace. If you are saved, you should be able to explain it in your own words. If you can't explain it, I doubt that you are saved. You do not need to go on a street corner to preach; mind you, I do not discourage those who do, it is their calling. If someone asks, plant the seed, (1 Peter 3:15).

Plant the seed and let God do the watering and growth. Take the example of the criminal who was hung on a cross adjacent to Jesus. He recognized that Jesus was Lord and believed all his heart that Jesus would be resurrected. Did he repent? Yes, he recognized that he was a sinner.

> *"But the other, answering, rebuked him, saying, "Do you not even fear God, seeing you are under the same condemnation? And we indeed justly, <u>for we receive the due reward of our deeds</u>; but this Man has done nothing wrong." Then he said to Jesus, "Lord, remember me when You come into Your kingdom,"* Luke 23:40-42

Watch this video which explains how simple the gospel was in the eyes of the criminal who hung adjacent to Jesus. "The Thief on the Cross (Pastor Charles Lawson)"

Watch this video which explains the mystery of "Where Did Jesus Go for Three Days and Three Nights after He was Crucified - Hank Lindstrom"

But what about our nation, what can we do?

The answer is for Christians to Stand on Guard for Thee - it is our duty - the Church is the Restrainer of lawlessness that is already at work until Christ calls the rapture, (2 Thess 2:7).

And for Canadians, believers or not, God is the pillar of our country... deny God and the pillar is removed...

> *"The nations have sunk down in the pit which they made; In the net which they hid, their own foot is caught,"* Psalm 9:15

> *"Draw near to God and He will draw near to you. Cleanse your hands, you sinners;*

and purify your hearts, you double-minded," James 4:8

Are you like Israel freshly out of Egypt? They complained and wanted to go back to Egypt, back to slavery in a sinful adultery country? Canada has sunk into the pit of lawlessness. Reform only starts from within the heart. Revival starts at the pulpit. The responsibility of the pastors, ministers and teachers is to teach the truth without holding back. The whole truth has been concealed by the church, intentionally or by deceit. Restoration of our nation also starts by being obedient to God's teaching and living by God's principals, (values) in our family, our neighbourhood, and all government institutions. Setting my heart in order became my top priority as I authored this book.

Martin Luther wrote thus of the universities, and I quote:

> "I am much afraid that the universities will be the great gates of hell unless they diligently labour in explaining the Holy Scriptures and engraving them in the hearts of youth. I advise no one to place his child where the Scriptures do not reign paramount. Every institution in which men are not unceasingly occupied with the word of God must become corrupt." page 86, The Great Controversy.

The Romanists (self-proclaimed elite) never lost grip of influence through the past centuries to the present. They have infiltrated the school system and universities through the Jesuit Order. Jesuits work in education, research, and cultural pursuits. Jesuits also organized retreats, minister in hospitals and parishes, sponsor direct social ministries, and promote ecumenical dialogue, unity among the church[47]. They have also infiltrated the reform churches through Freemasonry. Freemasonry, the recruiting agency luring innocent Christians into the fraternity of the Luciferian. Bit by bit, lie by lie, Christians fall away, and by the time they reach the 33 degrees order, they denied Jesus and Lucifer is accepted as lord and become members of the Shriners, "Ancient Arabic Order, Nobles of the Mystic Shrine." The Shriners (angel of light, 2 Corinthians 11:14) posing as good Samaritans that built and administered children's hospitals are just a bunch of deceitful clowns.

All Canadian institutions have been compromised, including all parties. I invite you to read my commentary titled, "Canada's Institutions Conquered"[48].

And what about the U.S.A.? It has been compromised since America gained its independence. Could it be that by 2035, America will be conquered by the Romanists[49]? As Canadians, we have received blessings and forgotten the blesser. Canadian baby boomers have had it easy since the Second World War thinking that the government's acting in your best interest. All Federal and Provincial parties, even municipalities are all in it. Freemasonry and Shriners members are everywhere. Watch this video which explains how _Freemason is dangerous cult[50]. Topical teaching discusses the overall practice of Freemasonry and how many in this well-known fraternity claim to be Christians while serving another master?

---

[47] https://www.simplicityinthegospel.com/2013/05/interfaith-gathering-of-tares.html
[48] https://www.simplicityinthegospel.com/2022/01/canadas-institutions-conquered.html
[49] https://vaticanassassins.org/2011/12/23/masonic-iluminiati-created-and-ruled-by-the-black-pope-and-select-high-jesuits/
[50] https://youtu.be/GrBEy2rzhvk

Should we throw away the white towel recognizing defeat? Absolutely not. We are so like the Israelites who on so many occasions faced unbeatable enemies. The Church has the responsibility to hold back Satan's wicked scheme for the purpose to save souls first and foremost. The truth must be proclaimed, must be made available no matter what the condition and circumstance of the nation finds itself.

The book, The Great Controversy, describes the political power the Romanists had over all the known kingdoms in Europe and shows how it was extremely challenging for Martin Luther.

> "Yet the mandate of Rome was not without effect. Prison, torture, and sword were weapons potent to enforce obedience. The weak and superstitious trembled before the decree of the pope; and while there was general sympathy for Luther, many felt that life was too dear to be risked in the cause of reform. Everything seemed to indicate that the Reformer's work was about to close." page 87, The Great Controversy.

To these threats, Luther wrote,

> "My enemies have been able, by burning my books, to injure the cause of truth in the minds of the common people, and destroy their souls; for this reason, I consumed their books in return. A serious struggle has just begun. Hitherto I have been only playing with the pope. I began this work in God's name; it will be ended without me, and by His might." page 87, The Great controversy.

No one in Canada has lived through a dictatorship such as suffered by Christians in China, and North Korea. Many warnings came from those who escaped to Canada. But it was ignored. The covid-19 fake pandemic has proven that most of the population easily submitted to coercion from The Hon. Trudeau mandates.

Under pressure, many gave away their freedom, for the sake of saving their wealth. Many took the untested vaccine believing that it would save their lives. Peter McCullough, MD, MPH expose the danger of the vaccine[51].

Many of my co-workers through the coercion of losing their job took the jab (vaccine). Many, as I have, were given leave without pay and suffered financial consequences, denied EI. My wife and I got in debt, moved to my daughter's basement, and are now liquidating our property investment. At 70 years old and my wife who is suffering an injury from a car accident with little compensation are living in faith and hope. We both made the right choice with no regret. Now statistics are out. There are reports of serious injuries and death among the vaccinated. Dr. Mike Yeadon report that they Lied About Everything, Including That There Was a Pandemic[52]

Is it worth fighting for a cause when 60% of the population favoured the government? Is it worth defending those who fear and submit to coercion? I have learned a lesson from my dad. He is a French Canadian and voluntarily joined the army before WWII conscription. That was very unusual. He joined an English infantry and fought in Sicily. He returned with no injury but suffered from a stomach ulcer. He died at

---

[51] https://rumble.com/vnbv86-winning-the-war-against-therapeutic-nihilism-and-trusted-treatments-vs-unte.html
[52] https://rumble.com/v1qztky-dr.-mike-yeadon-they-lied-about-everything-including-that-there-was-a-pande.html

55 years old. Why did he volunteer? He never told me. For honour and country? You might assume. For his family? He was single at the time. I watched in black and white many Second World War TV documentations with him, in silence, with no pause to explain what he went through. I figure that he volunteers because it was the right thing to do.

To my children, as they were growing up, I taught two principalities about taking responsibility. Responsibility is about admitting your wrongdoing. Responsibility is about taking the helm when no one else wants to.

Today, who would want to join the armed forces to defend the interest of these fascist groups of elites who control the U.N., and 194 nations for the purpose to take away your freedom of conscience, your time, your treasure, and your talent?

> *"You, therefore, my son, be strong in the grace that is in Christ Jesus. And the things that you have heard from me among many witnesses, commit these to faithful men who will be able to teach others also. You, therefore, must endure hardship as a good soldier of Jesus Christ,"* 2 Timothy 2:1-3

Remember for whom our veterans fought for

November the 11th, in Canada, we pause from all our activities for 2 minutes in remembrance of those who fought for our Rights and our Freedoms. Our military personnel fought for justice, against tyranny in foreign countries.

In a time of peace, we remember for whom our veterans fought. They fought for the next generation. They fought for our freedom against totalitarianism and oppression. They fought for our freedom to choose our destiny. They fought for our religious freedom. They fought for our right to make decisions for the benefit of our children's future according to our culture and tradition, and our values. Our veterans fought for our freedom to travel whenever and wherever we want to go within our borders. They fought for our freedom of speech and of writing commentaries, even when disrespectfully challenged by others, just as our opponents have the freedom to do so.

Us Christians we have dropped our guard and allowed the Canadian federal and provincial leaders to dictate what we are to accept culturally. Both levels of government have become autocratic to the core, under the umbrella of political correctness accusing Christians of intolerance and racism when Christians voiced their concerns. They use an imaginary virus, (well stage mine you) and climate change to subdue us to surrender our sovereign economy, our sovereign right to live free, and our sovereign parental duty toward our children. Only God has the sovereignty to control the weather, (Job 28:25-27, Psalm 148:8). Besides, the weather has been degenerating since the fall of man. What arrogant from these elites to play god.

> *"The wind blows where it wishes, and you hear the sound of it, but cannot tell where it comes from and where it goes. So is everyone who is born of the Spirit"* John 3:8

Not even a single gunshot has been fired

Our Rights and Freedoms cost the lives of many soldiers, pilots, and navy personnel. All were grieved by a loved one, from a father, a mother, a wife and children, a brother and a sister who will never be comforted for their loss. It was a war by hand-to-hand combat, by infantry, artillery fire, air to air combat, bombing deliberately on the civilian populations, battleship against battleships, merchant' vessels against submarines.

The cost in human life and resources for our children's freedom far exceeds our comprehension.

It was worth it. *"Greater love has no one than this, than to lay down one's life for his friends,"* John 15:13

I hope with all my heart that the content of this book reaches faithful men and women who will be able to teach others to surrender all to Christ our Lord and be willing to fight for all truth to prevail.

Martin Luther replied to the reproaches of his enemies who taunted him with the weakness of his cause, he answered:

> "Who knows if God has not chosen and called me and if they ought not to fear that, by despising me, they despise God Himself? Moses was alone at the departure from Egypt; Elijah was alone in the reign of King Ahab; Isaiah alone in Jerusalem; Ezekiel alone in Babylon… God never selected as a prophet either the high priest or any other great personage; but ordinarily, He chose low and despised men, once even the shepherd Amos.
>
> In every age, the saints have had to reprove the great, kings, princes, priests, and wise men, at the peril of their lives… I do not say that I am a prophet, but I say that they ought

> to fear precisely because I am alone and that they are many. I am sure of this, that the word of God is with me, and that it is not with them." The pope had threatened Luther with ex-communication if he did not recant, and the threat was now fulfilled." Page 87 The Great Controversy.

Today, freedom of speech and our freedom to protect our children is being taken away because we took freedom for granted. We let this freedom go astray to a point where many take this liberty to sin evermore.

Who would die for a sinful nation that pollutes the mind of our Christian children with the woke ideology and lifestyle behaviour in our school that goes against the parents' choices, and goes against God? Who would die for a sinful nation that allows murdering unborn babies for the sake of convenience? Yes, we have freedom of conscience, but not the freedom to kill. All murderers will be given accountability.

Who would die for the leaders of a nation who would choose to serve the interests of The United Nations' Agenda 21, selling out the sovereignty of our national economy - for the creation of a New World in Disorder? WHO?

Jesus would and did.

Last Call

To Canadian Christians, God is the pillar of our country... deny God and the pillar is removed...

> *"The nations have sunk down in the pit which they made; In the net which they hid, their own foot is caught,"* Psalm 9:15

> *"Therefore be zealous and repent. Behold, I stand at the door and knock. If anyone hears My voice and opens the door, I will come in to him and dine with him, and he with Me,"* Revelation 3:19-20.

Does anyone remember spending a few evenings with your friends at a local bar? (That was before my conversion). How many remember the last call, which was 15 minutes to closing time when the bartender would cry a loud 'last call' to take your last order?

As Laodiceans, we should be like the bartender. We are to shout the last call to redemption before the dreadful and terrible day of God's wrath. Not Satan's wrath but God's, (1 Thess 5:9, Col 3:6). The wrath of God is more serious for the self-proclaimed elite because they suppress the truth. This goes also to pastors, ministers and teachers who will receive the hidden truth of the 21st century who deny it and refuse to share it with their members.

> *"For the wrath of God is revealed from heaven against all ungodliness and unrighteousness of men, who suppress the truth in unrighteousness,"* Romans 1:18

There is a great misconception concerning the Laodiceans who are to stay in the lukewarm state of stagnancy and that they will not be part of the rapture. Far from the truth. Many are being woken up by Jesus' knocking at the door. We are in the wake of a great revival, the greatest in all the history of the Church. It is more prevalent in the U.S.A. Why is that? It is my view that there are many remnants from the Philadelphia church era "He who has the key of David, He who opens, and no one shuts, and shuts and no one opens" (Rev 3:7) that are reminding many pastors and Christians of the importance of getting involved in politics from behind their pulpits. Such as Dr. Andy Wood, YouTube presentation titled "The Pulpit Versus the Government".[53] Pastor Dean Odle, YouTube channel - Dean Odle for Governor[54], setting an example by running as Governor for the state of Alabama, he is a flat earth truther with a YouTube series title "The Sevenfold Doctrine of Creation"[55] that I encourage you to watch. Then there is Pastor Robert Dean, How Should We Vote Then?[56], Craig Northcott - District Attorney at the 14th Judicial District of the state of Tennessee, you can view his YouTube presentation in the title, "The Local Church's Role in Government"[57]. There are Christian movements all over America involved in their local government. One channel that I subscribed to and suggest you follow is https://rumble.com/c/AndWeKnow[58] in which the host keeps track of all Christian/political activity throughout the U.S.A. These men and pastors play a key role in knocking at the door.

> *"With men this is impossible, but with God all things are possible,"* Matthew 19:26

---

[53] https://youtu.be/iNdvTveD-k8
[54] https://www.youtube.com/channel/UCmh0C-1XAyvthMXQB3wt_Fg
[55] https://www.youtube.com/playlist?list=PLJdMH7D12j5OoD-rVSfd-Oh7Owwz0uNnzB
[56] https://www.youtube.com/playlist?list=PL1ZC-1HJaptxZxtaLlcd6lBC9Pfbay4dp
[57] https://youtu.be/_DRZ14A_QYI
[58] https://rumble.com/c/AndWeKnow

Many Canadians volunteer their time and talent for the causes of protecting our rights and freedoms, but without the Church, they cannot succeed.

> *"Therefore be zealous and repent. Behold, I stand at the door and knock. If anyone hears My voice and opens the door, I will come in to him and dine with him, and he with Me,"* Revelation 3:19-20.

The knocking at the door represents the pulpit. God often used signs in the past to get our attention. With Moses, it was the burning bush that had not been consumed by fire. It got his attention. In the era of the Church, God is using His word. It was so in all past reformations and revivals. Individuals, not like Moses who tried to talk himself out of it but individuals who accepted the call of duty. Moses after 40 years as a shepherd forgot the cry of misery from his brother the Israelites in Egypt. He forgot about the newborn male baby who was still being thrown into the Nile River. He forgot the hardship of slavery with all its physical abuse.

In Canada, the spirit of Moses' reluctance is prominent in many churches. Many pastors find excuses for not getting politically involved, while abortion (murder) never ceases. There are over 50 thousand children disappearing per year[59]. Teenager suicide report increasing. Are they victims of the woke ideology in school?

There are reports of women, men, and children[60] incarcerated in secret dark basement and chained, force to satisfy the perverted sexual appetite of their aggressor. Do you not hear their cries of fear and desperation? Have you not heard the

---

[59] https://missingkids.ca/en/missing-children-database/
[60] https://asiasociety.org/trafficking-children-prostitution-and-unicef-response

cries of the senior citizens in residence? I did, every time I visited my mother. Have you not heard the cry of a desperate father, mother crying out to God to help him/her provide for his/her family? Who viewed the movie about a former abortion industry worker "UNPLANNED". Who viewed the part where the worker assisted the abortion doctor who suck the life of a child fighting for his/her life, the unheard cry of desperation. I did. I still cannot get this image out of my mind. The worship of the idol god Moloch come to mind. Moloch became the Israelites god, and they practiced a cruel form of worship ceremony, which consists of a sacrificing ritual of their own infants for the purpose of purging their sins.

The infants would be presented as a live burnt offering in the arms of Moloch accompanied by loud instruments of all kinds to subdue the cries of the infants and tearful mother's agony. God hear the infant cry, do you?

Where are the Canadian pastors who would dare to speak out behind the pulpit? Where are the members encouraging their pastors to do so? Do you remember Jesus' teaching about a friend coming at midnight asking for bread? Although the lesson is about being persistent in our prayers, it is also about Jesus' persistence in knocking at our hearts.

> *"And He said to them, "Which of you shall have a friend, and go to him at midnight and say to him, 'Friend, lend me three loaves; for a friend of mine has come to me on his journey, and I have nothing to set before him'; and he will answer from within and say, 'Do not trouble me; the door is now shut, and my children are with me in bed; I cannot rise and give to you'? I say to you, though he will not rise and give to him be-*

> *cause he is his friend, yet because of his persistence he will rise and give him as many as he needs,"* Luke 11:5-8

Doesn't that reflect the Laodicean attitude toward their calling? '*Do not trouble me; the door is now shut.*' Jesus is at the door of the Western Christian Laodicean most lukewarm church in the entire world and knocking. Not only knocking but also shouting, '*If anyone hears My voice.*' And look at the response, '*I say to you, though he will not rise and give to him <u>because he is his friend</u>, yet because of his persistence he will rise and give him as many as he needs.*' My dear friends, this call is from 'The Voice,' to His temple, (1 Cor 3:16). Jesus' persistence, isn't that an act of grace?

Doesn't Jesus consider us as friends?

> *"No longer do I call you servants, for a servant, does not know what his master is doing; but I have called you friends, <u>for all things</u> that I heard from My Father I have made known to you,"* John 15:15

That is the biggest problem in most churches, they do not know what Jesus is doing. It is not taught. So many avoid teaching God's prophetic words. Jesus has shared with the Church everything pertaining to His great plan of salvation and the establishment of His Kingdom on earth through the Scriptures. You receive more privileges of God's plan than Daniel did, (Daniel 12:4, Rev 2:10).

Would you be among those who choose to open the door, repenting and becoming zealous, (Rev 3:19). Repenting first by following these instructions.

"If then you were raised with Christ, seek those things which are above, where Christ is, sitting at the right hand of God. Set your mind on things above, not on things on the earth. For you died, and your life is hidden with Christ in God. When Christ who is our life appears, then you also will appear with Him in glory.

Therefore, put to death your members which are on the earth: fornication, uncleanness, passion, evil desire, and covetousness, which is idolatry.

Because of these things the wrath of God is coming upon the sons of disobedience, in which you yourselves once walked when you lived in them."

"But now you yourselves are to put off all these: anger, wrath, malice, blasphemy, filthy language out of your mouth. Do not lie to one another, (being pretentious) *since you have put off the old man with his deeds, and have put on the new man who is renewed in knowledge <u>according to the image of Him</u> who created him, where there is neither Greek nor Jew, circumcised nor uncircumcised, barbarian, Scythian, slave nor free, but Christ is all and in all,"*

"Therefore, as the elect of God, holy and beloved, put on tender mercies, kindness, humility, meekness, longsuffering; bearing with one another, and forgiving one another, if anyone has a complaint against another; even as Christ forgave you, so you also must do. But above all these things put

on love, which is the bond of perfection. And let the peace of God rule in your hearts, to which also you were called in one body; and be thankful. Let the word of Christ dwell in you richly in all wisdom, teaching and admonishing one another in psalms and hymns and spiritual songs, singing with grace in your hearts to the Lord. And whatever you do in word or deed, do all in the name of the Lord Jesus, giving thanks to God the Father through Him," Col 3:1-17

Once hearts have been turned to our Lord, then we can get to work shouting "LAST CALL", blowing the trumpet, being a watchman on the wall, some as prophets to the kings and leaders of the world, some to share the gospel, some to take care of the orphans, the poor, the heart broken, the needy, the homeless and the widows, and some as shepherds and teachers to unite the churches all for the glory of God, (Eph 4:13).

As a prophet, the responsibility is to witness to the kings and leaders of the word, by writing to them, reminding them that it is our Lord that has established them,
(Hebrews 13:17, Romans 13:1), reminding them that "The great day of the Lord is near, (Zeph 1:14-18), and inviting them to accept Jesus as Lord. Take part in politics. Rebuke, correct, admonish leaders to govern in righteousness, they also have been deceived, (2 Timothy 3:16, Revelation 12:9). Protect, the poor, the needy, the orphans, the widows, and the unborn on death role (abortion). Get involved in all levels of government, (Psalm 68:5, Isaiah 58:6,).

Charitable Tax Exemption - A compromise with the devil

The greatest obstacle to the western churches is the compromise that keeps them from fulfilling the task of a prophet. The Charitable Tax exemption is the greatest compromise made with the government. Please read my blog titled "Charitable Tax Exemption - A Pact with The Devil.[61]" When a church is registered as a charitable organization it becomes non-partisan politically and is obliged to play by the CRA rules.

In other words, the churches are not allowed to influence the flocks in any way or form politically, cannot take part in political campaigns and cannot preach behind the pulpit in favour of or against a political party, or party policy. And that my fellow Canadian Christians, is how the churches have been snared, keeping the Church from being a lamp, and salt.

That is how Canadian Christians have become doormats trampled underfoot by the federal and provincial governments. That is how we have lost our parental sovereignty over our children. We brought these conditions on ourselves for the sake of saving money on taxes. The corporate church wrote a pack with Satan. Churches have agreed in exchange for Tax exemption to waive their right to take part in any partisan political activity which involves direct or indirect support of or opposition to, any political party or candidate for public office. Under the devil's pact, a church denomination cannot single out the voting pattern on an issue of any elected representative or politician. We tend to be neutral, not to offend anyone for the fear of losing membership and

---

[61] https://www.simplicityinthegospel.com/2018/10/charitable-tax-exemption-pack-with-devil.html

therefore financial support. The freedom of conscience which was previously secured has now become vulnerable.

What does Jesus have to say about this pact?

> *"No servant can serve two masters; for either he will hate the one and love the other, or else he will be loyal to the one and despise the other. You cannot serve God and mammon,"* Luke 16:13

> *"Render therefore to Caesar the things that are Caesar's, and to God the things that are God's,"* Matt 22:21

Aren't our children worth much more than a Tax Exemption? Isn't freedom of conscience worth much more than Tax Exemption? Is it not time to get out of this curse that is destroying our Judeo-Christian culture in this once great nation? The churches have lost their salt flavors (its purpose) and the light on the lampstand has diminished our social and political influence. It is time we get involved; don't you think? Do not just vote for the less of all evil but vote according to your convictions. Promote and vote for the candidate that represents God's values. Vote by faith <u>and</u> conviction. Remember the miracle of The Multiplication of Bread and Fish, (Matthew 14:13-21). Vote righteously and let God do the rest.

The reality check-
We are against the greatest cult

Who is behind the entire global elite? The politicians, the bankers, the pharmaceutical industry, the legal institutions, the media, the entertainment industry, the high technology... they are but stooges, deceived and proud poppets.

Who is the master like-minded other than Lucifer? Who is the one who follow Satan instructions, the high commander. All world kingdoms are subdued by him. That include the pope, the kings, the politicians, all bank institution, the pharmaceutical industry, the legal institutions, the media, the entertainment industry, high technology, NASA, CFR, the FBI, CIA, the RCMP, CSIS, the British Institute of International Affairs, and The Unites Nation. Is it beyond the Romanist? Who hold all the king's captive. According to Daniel 2:21, it is God who removed and establish the kingship. Who is playing God?

The era of kings, monarchy has been replaced with a corporation era, where those who control the banks control all aspect of all nations. They control the mind, making you believe that you are part of an infinite universe, with an insignificant destiny. Yes, the kings are held captive just as they were by the Romanist and will be until Jesus return, (Rev 17:18). At Jesus return to establish His Kingdom, the kings of the earth will bow to Him, (Psalm 72:11). The kings of the earth still play an important role in bible prophecy.

We are dealing with a mind like Moa, a tyrant like Stalin, an occultist dictator like Hitler, all combined with a regime of the secret police, secret trials, and secret execution of whistleblowers, of secret assassination such as of President J.F. Kennedy. Sex, extortion, and bribe are used to extort and/or threat judges, politicians, and many men/women of great of influence of losing their lives or of loved one if they do not comply. How do you control a leader? How do you control a country? Who is responsible for the ruination and destruction of a peaceful nation such as Iraq, Afghanistan, and Libya just for the sake of protecting their currency, the Petrodollars, and least we forget 9/11 Twine Tower destruction? All leaders of the western world are guilty of indescribable atrocities, crimes against humanity. See what these puppets are planning: Digital ID[62]

Watch the untold story of Muammar Gaddafi.[63] The political leaders force the press, and the media into the cold, and all you will get is lies and innuendo, and nothing is worse for a free society than a media in service to the elite Luciferians and their stooge's politicians. It is Satan goal to eliminate Christians and atheists alike. His followers are witches and pedophiles, taking part in perverted ritual ceremonies. They called themselves illuminati. Who is the grand master behind the illuminate? It is beyond the House of Rockchild the founder of the international bankers, the guardian of the Vatican treasures, the Knights of Malta. Follow the money as a detective would say. It will take you to Satan's stooge, (Rev 17:5).

Message to the kings of the earth.

Jesus King of kings is your Lord, the ruler over the kings of the earth, (Rev 1:5). God took your kingdom away from you and made it a merely corporation number control by the Romanist, (Isaiah 14:12). As it happens to king Nebuchadnezzar, God temporarily take away your authority over your kingdom, (Dan 4:25), *"till you know that the Most High rules in the kingdom of men and gives it to whomever He chooses."*

Daniel message to king Nebuchadnezzar is for you also, *"break off your sins by being righteous, and your iniquities by showing mercy to the poor,"* Dan 4:27. *"Perhaps there may be a lengthening of your prosperity."*

---

[62] https://rumble.com/embed/v1jpayu/?pub=4
[63] https://youtu.be/HjmJHLanY3M

To the western churches

Sadly, and shamefully the churches have traded their soul to the devil, in as much as the Bohemians made concessions and compromises with Rome so have the modern corporate churches.

Who remembers the 2018 Summer Jobs Attestation? To be eligible, applicants had to attest that both the job and the organization's core mandate respect individual human rights in Canada, including the values underlying the Canadian Charter of Rights and Freedoms as well as other rights. These include reproductive rights, and the right to be from discrimination on the basis of sex, religion, race national or ethnic origin, colour, mental, or physical disability, <u>Sexual Orientation, or Gender Identity or Expression.</u>

This deceptive Thesis, Antithesis, Synthesis ruse is an orchestrated plot by all Canadian political parties whose agenda is the globalization of our nation, to prepare a worldwide military appraisal against Christians. The unbelievers feel in their bones that something bad is about to happen and feel helpless, while the church has all the resources available in the word of God, with the power to control evil, (Matt 28:18). I invite you to read from my blog an article titled, "Deceptive Ruse - Thesis, Antithesis, Synthesis[64]"

Example of past concession

The Bohemians were successful against the Romanists' continuous attacks of aggression securing the freedom of conscience.

Quoting from the book, "The Great Controversy" on page 70

---

[64] https://www.simplicityinthegospel.com/2018/12/deceptive-ruse-thesis-antithesis_20.html

"The papal leaders, despairing of conquering by force, at last resorted to diplomacy. A compromise was entered into, that while professing to grant the Bohemians freedom of conscience, really betrayed them into the power of Rome. The Bohemians had specified four points in Rome: the free preaching of the Bible; the right of the church to both the bread and the wine in the communion, and the use of the mother tongue in divine worship; the exclusion of the clergy from all secular offices and authority; and, in cases of crime, the jurisdiction of the civil courts over clergy and laity alike. The papal authorities at last "agreed that four articles of the Hussites should be accepted, but that the right of explaining them, which is of determining their precise import, should belong to the council - in other words, the pope and the emperor." On this basis, a treaty was entered into, and Rome gained by dissimulation and fraud what she failed to gain by conflict; for, placing her interpretation upon the Hussite articles, as upon the Bible, she could pervert their meaning to suit her own purposes."

Nothing new under the sun comes to mind. The same tactic was used to undermine Canadian citizens and the churches. The Canadian Federal government instituted the Canadian Human Rights Commission to supersede The Charter of Rights and Freedoms which was written in simple language for Canadians to understand. Therefore, the federal government turned and twisted the simplicity of The Charter of Rights and Freedoms into a complex and confusing vocabulary to persuade the average Canadian to let THEM - the government take charge to define every aspect of the constitution, making it powerless for all Canadians. The government defines every aspect of the constitution, making it powerless for all Canadians.

Prior to The Charter of Rights and Freedoms the Federal government under the Liberal leadership of Hon. Pierre E. Trudeau established in 1977 The Charter of Rights and Freedoms under a new institution, namely The Human Right Commission. You would probably believe that the Human Rights Commission would side with Judeo-Christian values, but aux-contrary, it sided with humanism philosophies founded by the human ethical belief that we are all equal to our belief without God of the Bible in the picture. It will be utilized as the tools of reason, based on science and human logic when approaching problem-solving and constitutional decision making.

What were the consequences? Christians were now vulnerable since the government through the Human Rights Commission was making up the rules on our behalf without shepherds to defend them. The Charter is entrenched by LAW in the Constitution of Canada, therefore unmovable, as for the Canadian Human Rights Act, however, is simply a piece of federal legislation, which may be repealed or revised by a simple majority vote in the federal House of Commons. In simple language, the federal government installed a window blind in front of the Constitution so that average Canadians, particularly Christians would not have access to the light (the truth).

From then on, it did not get any better. In 1996, for example, the Act was amended through the Human Rights Commission to include sexual orientation as an enumerated ground of discrimination. As such, the Act now prohibits discrimination on the grounds of a person's sexuality. The sad result is that Christian parents, and all other parents of different religions, cultures, traditions, and moral values are powerless from the constant attack from the school boards all over Canada, supported by the Canadian Human Rights Act to teach sexual behaviours that go against parents' consent. The government owns our children – the United Nations owns children through the Canadian International Development Agency (CIDA).

Please read my two articles that cover the subject in detail on my web page, here is the title and the link;

CANADIAN CHARTER OF RIGHTS AND FREEDOMS VS THE CANADIAN HUMAN RIGHTS COMMISSION[65]

Charitable Tax Exemption - A Pact With The Devil[66]

Message from Dr. Jordan B Peterson to the global elites:

Excerpt from an article in the UK The Telegraph

"Back Off, Oh Masters of the Universe"

> "So, leave us alone, you centralizers of power, you worshipers of Gaia, you did sacrifices of the wealth and property of others, you would be planetary saviours, you Machiavellian pretenders and virtue signalers objecting to power, all the while you gathered around you madly."
>
> "Leave us alone, to prosper or not as a result of our own choices as a result of our own actions in the exercise of our own requisite and irreducible responsibility"

---

[65] https://www.simplicityinthegospel.com/2019/02/canadian-charter-of-rights-and-freedoms.html
[66] https://www.simplicityinthegospel.com/2018/10/charitable-tax-exemption-pack-with-devil.html

The link:
"Leave us alone or reap the whirlwind"[67]

Globalist utopians demand that we fall in line with their "cure" for climate change. Dr Jordan B Peterson explains why the goal of achieving net zero emissions by 2050 is absolutely preposterous.

Uk The Telegraph Article titled "Peddlers of environmental doom have shown their true totalitarian colours"[68]

What is behind these elite's goal to bring about a New World In-Disorder? In my view, it is a plot to bring into submission the whole world for a common goal, to prepare a worldwide revolt against The Lord, The King, and The Creator Jesus our Christ at His return, (Psalm 2:1-3)

Duties of a member of the body of Christ
All deck on hands

Canada is in a great state of spiritual emergency. The enemies of God are ready to execute their agenda for their fantasy utopia of new world in dis-order. They have not read the Bible which foretells their failure. Satan has deceived his followers as he did toward one-third of God's angels. There is nothing new about Satan's plan. His plan will fail as it as in the days of Noah, and as it failed at the construction of the tower of Babel. His agenda always brings chaos, disorder, and ruins. Sadly, Canadian citizens are blinded and limited in being dissatisfied with their government.

---

[67] https://youtu.be/--QS_UyW2SY
[68] https://www.telegraph.co.uk/news/2022/08/15/peddlers-environmental-doom-have-shown-true-totalitarian-colours/

Few recognize the power scheme that originated from these Luciferian' elites. Canadian citizens believe that "We the people" are the ones who can disrupt their plan without recognizing that we are against powerful enemies in the spiritual realm. We have seen many examples in the Old Testament when Israel was defeated by their enemies for not acknowledging God first and neglecting to consult Him. So, it is in every nation. People are taking a stand against the elites without knowing that their enemy is the great Lucifer. His followers are everywhere. They have been recruited through the Freemasons, the Knights of Columbus, the Shriners, Skull and Bones, and many not-so-secret societies, and least we ignore, the new age cult. For their allegiance, they receive fame, wealth, sex, and success in all aspects of their life. It has been promised and delivered. Once they realize to whom they have allegiance, they are fearful of losing their lives if they leave, believing that since they have sold their soul to Satan there is no way out. That is a lie. Your soul belongs to God and Satan knows that. There is a way out and it is through Jesus. Please read this article titled, "Have You Traded Your Soul? Is It A Done Deal?[69]"

There is a time of great persecution coming against the church. There is nowhere to flee as it was during the early church persecution in Jerusalem (Acts 4:1). There are many Canadians with American citizenships who are returning to the U.S.A. thinking that they will avoid persecution. In a near future, it is inevitable for no matter where Christians flee, there will be persecution.

---

[69] https://www.simplicityinthegospel.com/2012/12/have-you-traded-your-soul.html

Therefore, it is urgent as a member of the body of Christ, that we share the gospel of hope and actively be involved in politics. Give your time, your treasures, and your talents to God. Avoid being like 'Moses' who tried to talk his way out when God spoke to him through a burning bush. Moses gave all kinds of excuses to avoid his call of duty to save his own kind who were under harsh conditions. If not saved, all men and women created in the image of God are slaves to Satan's deception. Talk to your pastor and share the content of this book. Share with all your Christian friends. Take part in a group which has the same inspiration to serve the Lord. Pray, pray, pray with a sense of urgency.

> *"For I am not ashamed of the gospel of Christ, for it is the power of God to salvation for everyone who believes, for the Jew first and also for the Greek,"* Romans 1:16
>
> *"But as we have been approved by God to be entrusted with the gospel, even so, we speak, not as pleasing men, but God who tests our hearts,"* 1 Thess 2:4.
>
> *"And have no fellowship with the unfruitful works of darkness, but rather expose them... But all things that are exposed are made manifest by the light, for whatever makes manifest is light."* Eph 5:11,13

Be led by the Holy Spirit as Phillip has been to answer the spiritual curiosity of the Ethiopian eunuch, (Acts 8:26-40).

Be prepared to face an enemy of the Church such as Justin Trudeau, to bring him/her to the Lord. The story of Paul's conversion highlights the role that Ananias played in cultivating Paul's encounter and entrance into a relationship with God, (Acts 9:1-25).

Most important, support your pastor by praying for him and supporting him continually with encouraging words. Pastors do a lot to encourage the many who have life challenges and to those who need guidance. Please do the same for him on all occasions. Support your local church financially, if possible, by not claiming tax exemption, or request that the CRA clause of non-political involvement be removed. Take the example of unions and syndicates, they are allowed to influence their members in any way or form politically, to take part in political campaigns and to stand in favour of a political party, or party policy.

Duty of Pastors

As good shepherds and teachers, you have the responsibility to teach all things without holding back any truth. Verse by verse, chapter by chapter, book by book, and especially the words of prophecy, (1 Cor 14:1).

> *"And moreover, because the Preacher was wise, he still taught the people knowledge; yes, he pondered and sought out and set in order many proverbs. The Preacher sought to find acceptable words; and what was written was upright words of truth. The words of the wise are like goads, and the words of scholars are like well-driven nails, given by one Shepherd. And further, my son, be admonished by these. Of making many books there is no end, and much study is wearisome to the flesh,"* Eccl 12:9-12

The call of a teacher comes with great responsibilities. Every word coming out of his mouth will be accounted for. He cannot slack off teaching the truth, (Mark 13:33-37, Luke

12:40). What can the flock learn in a 10-minute pamphlet prepared sermon?

We all have a key role within the body of Christ, seeking God's knowledge and direction in our life. The pastor's duty is to prepare and equip all of the saints to do different functions of stewardship in the ministry and to prepare everyone for our inheritance in the position of governance within the kingdom of God.

> *"And He Himself gave some to be apostles, some prophets, some evangelists, and some pastors and teachers, for the equipping of the saints for the work of ministry, for the edifying of the body of Christ, till we all come to the unity of the faith and of the knowledge of the Son of God, to a perfect man, to the measure of the stature of the fullness of Christ,"* Eph 4:11-13

Do not slack off supporting your pastor. It is lonely at the top.

The Doctrine of the Rapture - Hindering the duty of a steward

There are many Christians who believe in the pre-tribulation rapture as I do. But instead of being occupied by fulfilling their role of a steward, they are just sitting around with their arms crossed and waiting for the event to happen. Are you one of them? The more the popularity of the doctrine of the rapture increases, the more Christians conclude that since we are guaranteed to escape God's wrath, there is nothing to do but to kill time. Many are not upset and outraged at the increase of sin and injustice in their neighbourhood, nation, and the world. Many do not overcome personal sins and do not strive to become Holy as Jesus is Holy. I am still talking to the Laodicean church era,

Many do not bother to share the gospel of salvation with anyone. Many think they are saved but are not. Many do not take care of widows and orphans or visit prisoners. Many do not visit the sick and take time to look after the homeless. Too many stay-at-home Christians do not even show up to church services to mingle with Christians. Many do not take time to fellowship with God in prayers and Bible study. Too many observe pagan holidays, Christmas, Halloween, and Easter, lying to their children. Santa Clause, the easter bunny, and the tooth fairy do not exist. Please read my commentary title; "Merry Christmas or Happy Holiday?[70]"

Some Christian makes an annual offering, which they conclude is sufficient to guarantee a ticket to heaven. Can you tell the difference between a Christian and a humanist? The difference is that a humanist loves his neighbour and do good in the society without God in the picture. Does this describe the Laodicean Church era of which I also am part? I plead guilty to all these charges. I do not qualify to author this article, but someone must. I am sharing what I needed to learn. There was no burning bush appearance, there was no vision, no dream, no voice therefore I cannot say "Thus says the Lord God." I was convicted by the Word. His word (the Bible) compelled me to write this admonition, this exultation. The Holy Spirit has everything to do with this.

As for the rapture, it is the doctrine of eminency. That means, expect Jesus to return for His Bride the Church between <u>now and then</u> He will appear. I call it the prophecy of now and then. There are no signs of prophecy that will give a hint of

---

[70] https://www.simplicityinthegospel.com/2014/11/merry-christmas-or-happy-holiday.html

when and how it will come about, none! It is a promise made by Jesus to His disciples, (John 14:1-4). The waiting started when Jesus ascended to heaven, (Luke 24:51). The waiting stopped when He appeared, (1 Thess 4:16-18).

There is only one clue; it will happen before the antichrist comes into the world and that is so broad in time. Not even (2 Thessalonians 2:3), *"for that Day will not come unless the falling away comes first"*. The falling away is defined as defection from truth (properly the state), ("apostasy"): - falling away, forsake, G646. The falling away from the true gospel started immediately when Caesar Constantinople converted to Christianity, proclaiming Christianity as Rome's national religion. Satan plans to deceive throughout the centuries. His plan was described in the book, 'The Great Controversy.

> "Satan, therefore, laid his plan to war successfully against the government of God by planting his banner in the Christian church. If the followers of Christ could be deceived and lead the displease God, then their strength, fortitude, and firmness would fail and would fall an easy prey." page 18.

> "Most of the Christians, at last, consented to lower their standard, and a union was formed between Christianity and paganism," page 18

> "Thus, as long as persecution continued, the church remained comparatively pure. But as it ceased, converts were added who were less sincere and devoted, and the way was open for Satan to obtain a foothold," page 19.

That is when the falling away started, it was ongoing, and keep on going. It is not from yesterday that Satan used the tactic of infiltration. We have seen it through Israel's history, and we are seeing it today within the churches. The so-called not-so-secret societies namely the Cabal, the Freemasons, the Shriners, known as the Ancient Arabic Order of the Nobles of the Mystic Shrine, and the Jesuits Romanist steward have infiltrated the churches. No pulpit dares to expose them. No pulpit dares to disallow them from being in the assembly.

> *"And have no fellowship with the unfruitful works of darkness, but rather expose them,"* Ephesians 5:11

Now, look at the result. Churches no matter how much they live according to the simplicity of Christ have failed to live in the simplicity in Christ, walking with Jesus. Go figure that one out.

> "Satan exalted that he had succeeded in deceiving so large a number of the followers of Christ. He then brought his power to bear more fully upon these and inspired them to persecute those who remained true to God," page 19

There are over 63 versions of the Bible in circulation. Except for a few, all have corrupted the words. The most successful deception of all was denying God as the Creator, although it is clearly stated, "In the beginning God created the heavens and the earth,"

> "The great apostate had succeeded in exalting himself, *"above all that is called God, or that is worshiped,"* (2 Thess 2:4).
>
> He dared to change the only precept of the divine law that unmistakably points all mankind to the true and living God. In the fourth commandment, <u>God is revealed as the Creator of heavens and the earth and is thereby distinguished from all false God</u>, (page 26)

This is a crucial point to remember which will be discussed later.

The falling away

> *"For the mystery of lawlessness is already at work; only He who now restrains will do so until He is taken out of the way,"* 2 Thess 2:7

The falling away started even during Jesus' ministry. At one time there were more than twelve disciples following Jesus. We know the exact number were seventy disciples, (Luke 10:17). After listening to Jesus' teaching about eating His flesh and drinking His blood, all left except for the original disciples.

> *"Whoever eats My flesh and drinks My blood has eternal life, and I will raise him up at the last day. For My flesh is food indeed, and My blood is drink indeed,"*
> Jn 6:55-56

> *"From that time many of His disciples went back and walked with Him no more,"* v66

You can view my commentary titled, "The Unbelievers"[71] in my blogs.

As for the event called the rapture no one knows except Jesus, the Father, and the Holy Ghost. It could happen before or after the destruction of Damascus, it could happen before or after the war of Gog and Magog against Israel. The appearance of the anti-Christ could happen immediately after the war of Gog and Magog against Israel, or 100 years after.

---

[71] https://www.simplicityinthegospel.com/2014/04/john-666.html

All we know is that the antichrist will appear on the world scene only after the Church is taken away. The rapture could happen during a Jewish feast day or may not. The bottom-line, we are to be looking for Christ and not for the antichrist. I love studying prophecy, from many teachers, after all the reward is a blessing, I go by being a student of Bible prophecy, not a teacher. (Revelation 1:3). The study of prophecy always points out God's agenda, not Satan's.

Here is the basic instruction I recommend we must do until Jesus returns. I call them "The three Bs"

- Be watchful
- Be ready
- Be working

What is Satan after, after all?

Our Freedom of Consciousness - Free will

> *"I call heaven and earth as witnesses today against you, that I have set before you life and death, blessing and cursing; therefore, choose life, that both you and your descendants may live; "that you may love the Lord your God, that you may obey His voice, and that you may cling to Him, for He is your life and the length of your days; and that you may dwell in the land which the Lord swore to your fathers, to Abraham, Isaac, and Jacob, to give them,"* Deuteronomy 30:19-20

Isn't the Church grafted into Israel's olive tree? There is a saying "what's good for the goose is good for the gander"

> *"For if God did not spare the natural branches, He may not spare you either.*

Therefore consider the goodness and severity of God: on those who fell, severity; but toward you, goodness, if you continue in His goodness. Otherwise, you also will be cut off," Romans 11:21-22

The objective of these verses is to indicate that God has given us freedom of conscience, - free will. Whether as believers or not, we both have the freedom to make choices. But once becoming redeemed, we enter into the family of God, and as a good Father, He will correct us for drifting away from Him as He did to Israel. He is doing this for our own good.

Israel's enemies are our enemies. The enemies have the same goal and that is to take away our God's given freedom of conscience, and freedom to walk in the righteousness of God, therefore attempting to diminish our influence (light) in the society. Satan already has and still has in the palms of his hand the unbelievers under his influence of deception, (Rev 12:9). Unfortunately, the unbelievers do not see God's grace at work in their life Who is trying to save them from Satan's ruse.

Like many reformers, I also was born and raised in a pool of lies. I received my education in the Roman Catholic institution during my first eight grades. I therefore lived under the Romanist traditions with all their superstitious observations. Their goals were to push people away from God, and they successfully achieved that goal in the 20th century when the sex scandal with young children was exposed. In the past, it was covered up by the papacies. The Catholic church attendants now trickled to a bare minimum, but in my view the Romanist economic and geo-political influence had gained greater influence since the agreement between Hitler and the papacy.

You can view the agreement in this article titled; "The Vatican Concordat With Hitler's Reich: The Concordat of 1933 was ambiguous in its day and remains so."[72]

The Heavens Declare the Glory of God
The Hidden Truth Disclosed

"The heavens declare the glory of God, and the firmament shows His handiwork,"
Psalm 19:1

In the book of Psalm, chapter 19 expresses the perfect revelation of the Lord, His glory. The creation of the heavens and earth is a constant reminder that God is Sovereign, thereby distinguished from all false gods. The sun, the moon, and the stars have been created for signs and seasons, and for days and years, (Gen 1:14). Many, if not most Christian denominations do not believe in the literal description of how the creation came about and how we humans follow. It is viewed by some as a metaphor, some view it as a fairy tale story for children and some mix it with science, theory, and truth. Very few take Genesis 1:6 literally, and if they do, they are viewed as mentally out of order.

Even those who profess the Bible to be true, endorsing the inerrancy of the word of God, free from error, and exempt from error are skeptical of some aspects of how the creation came about. I have in my library a book titled; Vital Issues in the Inerrancy Debate, which contains 563 pages where the editor made an in-depth study defending the infallibility of the word of God, yet he would not accept all of Genesis

---

[72] https://www.americamagazine.org/faith/2003/09/01/vatican-concordat-hitlers-reich-concordat-1933-was-ambiguous-its-day-and-remains

chapter one literally. Many think that I am pushing the pen a bit too far. You may be stating that it really does not matter. After all, we are saved by grace through faith in our Lord Jesus. Believing that the blue sky above is water is irrelevant, it does not matter.

Why should it matter?

Satan is aware that discrediting God as the Creator of all things as described in the first chapter of Genesis will cause many to deny God's existence, therefore will not fear God, will not repent, and will not accept Jesus as their Savior. Since they do not believe in a creation made by God, they conclude that hell does not exist either.

> *"The secret things belong to the Lord our God, but those things which are revealed belong to us and to our children forever, that we may do all the words of this law,"* Deuteronomy 29:29

When the truth is replaced by a lie from one generation it is forgotten in all following generations, and it becomes a myth. Throughout past centuries the true gospel of salvation has been hidden by the Romanists who fail to preach it. Persecution was made against those who exposed them as liars, who profit financially by imposing a yoke to attain salvation. The Romanists made the true way to salvation a secret. Through the ruse of deception, fear, and collusion, the Romanists are guilty of sending billions to hell. Do you now understand what stirred up the flame in the heart of all the reformers to whom God revealed the secret things that belong to the Lord? The secret revealed by the reformers was.

> *Jesus said to him, "I am the way, the truth, and the life. No one comes to the Father except through Me,"* John 14:6

> *"For by grace you have been saved through faith, and that not of yourselves; it is the gift of God, not of works, lest anyone should boast,"* Eph 2:8-9

Nowadays, what is the secret which belongs to God that causes many to reject Jesus and end up in hell? It is rejecting God as the Creator, as The Father. Not only His creation is not acknowledged by the secular, but some aspects of God's creation are rejected by Christians. Satan through the ruse of pseudo-science, (theory of evolution, the big bang) has successfully deceived not only the secular but Christians as well.

> *"By faith, we understand that the worlds were framed by the word of God so that the things which are seen were not made of things which are visible,"* Hebrews 11:3

Christians believe in Jesus' resurrection through the testimony of His disciples, (John 17:20-21), by faith, not by sight., yet do not believe the evidence which is visible to their eyes that the blue sky above is water as described in (Genesis 1:6).

The Deceiver at Work

> *"The coming of the lawless one is according to the working of Satan, with all power, signs, and lying wonders,"* 2 Thess 2:9

> *"For false christs and false prophets will rise and show signs and wonders to deceive, if possible, even the elect,"* Mark 13:22

The coming of the lawless one was in the making since Jesus ascended to heaven. All power through lies and deceptions was used by the authority of the Romanists. Now, the modern-day magic of technology makes it easy to create signs to deceive.

> *"For in it the righteousness of God is revealed from faith to faith; as it is written, "The just shall live by faith,"* Romans 1:17

My parents raised me in the Roman Catholic tradition. I attended a catholic school. I was an altar boy, regularly scheduled to assist the priest serving mass. It was all in Latin then. There were a lot of rituals, lots of ceremonies and strict observances. It was all about work keeping my salvation, which continuously reminded me of the fear of hell. A door-to-door salesman knocked at my door one day at the age of 20. Without any hesitation, I asked if he had a Bible. That is when I became in love with the truth. In those days it was forbidden for Catholic members to own a Bible, especially with the full Old Testament version. I was fascinated even if I could not understand. It was a long journey, I made mistakes. Eventually, I started to read the Bible, taking it, as is, by taking Jesus by His word. What makes God's word difficult to understand? We tend to view the Bible from a secular point of view. I was born in an ocean of lies, bit by bit I learned to distinguish the lies.

Isn't faith a decision to believe, an action to take God by His word as Abel, Enoch, Noah, and Abraham did? When I come across a verse which is difficult to believe, I ask what lies interfere with my understanding? Often, I find myself like the Ethiopian on his way back home who needed help to understand, (Isaiah 53). God sent Philip to help him, (Acts 8:26). I read commentaries, and listened to many MP3s, and videos from many teachers. They were my Philips helping me to understand God's word. Especially if there is no Bible church in the area. Studying God's words will most likely challenge us to decide to believe, to trust God's word.

Everything you need to know about God is found in the Holy Scriptures. God reveals to those who diligently seek Him. So why should we not believe God as the author of the creation as described in the Book of Genesis Chapter one? Is it not reinforcing God's existence in this world and in our lives? Inasmuch as the rainbow reminds us that God keeps His promise, the blue sky above is water just as described in Genesis 1:6 remind us that God's thrown is nearby.

> *"Then God said, "Let there be a firmament in the midst of the waters, and let it divide the waters from the waters."*

Firmament is described as in the Strong Concordance from H7554; property an expanse that is, the firmament or (apparently) <u>visible arch of the sky</u>: - firmament.

In Ezekiel 1:26 in the Easy-to-Read Version, God's throne location is described as such.

> *"There was something that looked like a throne on top of the bowl. It was blue like sapphire. There was also something that looked like a man sitting on the throne."*

Everything about this blue planet is a lie for the purpose to push you away from God. The truth is, the earth is flat, you live in a dome, you are alone in the universe since there is no universe and since the universe does not exist, the conclusion is that there is one true God, you were not created by luck, by the goddess of providence, (Providentia).

Napoleon Bonaparte said, *"I am the instrument of Providence, she will use me as long that I accomplish her design, then she will break me like a glass."* And she did, didn't she?

The sooner you accept the truth the sooner you will feel liberated and free from the traps of deceptions. It is frightening to realize that the Bible is true and that you will be giving account for your sinful actions. By the grace of God, He made salvation so easily accessible that you only need to accept Jesus as Lord and believe with all your heart that He was resurrected to receive the gift of eternal life, (Romans 10:9).

To know more about how easy it is, please read my article titled, "When Did I Receive The Gift of Eternal Life?"[73] in my blog.

Signs of Wonders

Moses was who God gave authority of Himself to Pharaoh to liberate His people, Israel. God demonstrated His existence and His authority through many plagues on the people of Egypt, but it took a lot of convincing especially to Pharaoh. In verse nine of chapter seven, Pharaoh requests Moses to show him a sign, and a miracle so that he may know who sent him. He did not ask so that he may believe, but merely to understand with whom, which god with whom he (Pharaoh) was dealing. According to Pharaoh, He could be dealing with charlatans, impostors, and sorcerers. Aaron's first sign as instructed by God was to cast down his rod before Pharaoh and it became a serpent.

> *"But Pharaoh also called the wise men and the sorcerers; so the magicians of Egypt, also did in like manner with their enchantments. For every man threw down his rod, and they became serpents,"* Ex1:11-12.

As you can see, Pharaoh was wise to ask for proof of Moses' authority. Pharaoh is not so gullible. After seeing that his servants were capable of doing the same signs, he glowed

---

[73] https://www.simplicityinthegospel.com/2013/10/when-did-i-receive-gift-of-eternal-life.html

with pride in his wisdom. It was only a short victory since Aaron's rod swallowed up their snakes. The result was that Pharaoh's heart grew hard, and he did not heed with understanding. Egypt strong military influence in the surrounding nations was its strong economy generated by cheap labor, mainly from the children of Israel.

Today, churches do not need to prove who God is to the world's leaders. The world leaders know that the water above is water as described in Gen 1:6. They hide the truth from the world population. The Antarctic Treaty was signed in Washington on December 1st, 1959, by the twelve countries, now fifty-four. The US and Russia maintain a "basic territorial claim." The treaty was made under the ruse of Environmental Protection. As all national leaders, Hon. Justin Trudeau knows that the earth is flat. That is what makes these self-proclaimed elites and leaders so arrogant by knowing something that you do not. They are so haughty, that it is on display at the United Nations.

The Honourable Marc Garneau, astronaut has never been to space, just like The General Governor Julie Payette.

> *"For there is nothing covered that will not be revealed, nor hidden that will not be known,"* Luke 12:2

United Nation is destroying the U.S.A. The enemy within Watch; The Illuminati and CFR Speech by Myron C. Fagan (1967).[74]

We were born in an ocean of lies. Take Jesus walking on water as an analogy, (not a metaphor, not as an allegory, and neither as a typology). Jesus walks above the lies for it is impossible for Him to sink into the lies, (Hebrews 6:18). Peter asked Him if he could join Him. Jesus replied "come." As long as Peter looked at Jesus, the living truth, he walked above the lies. But his eyes started to focus on the lies, (he doubts) he sank, panicked, and asked for help. Jesus pulled him out of the lies and said to him, *"O you of little faith, why did you doubt?"* (Matt 14:31).

---

[74] https://www.bitchute.com/video/JC8MBjJcLxkS/

Why don't Christians accept Gen 1:6 as truth? It is because we refuse to take a leap of faith and to prove it validity. We learn to swim, to live partially above the water (the lies) just as Peter did, (John 21:7). The leaders of nations do not <u>believe</u> that God exists, <u>they know</u> that He exists, but they defy Him.

God Delusion vs. Satan's Deceit

God has sent a **strong delusion**, (2 Thess 2:10-13) that they should believe the lie. Why would a loving God create a delusion? *"Because they did not receive the love of the truth, that they might be saved."* The book to the Thessalonians was written around 51–52 AD, shortly after the First Epistle. Therefore, it was not a prophecy for our time. This delusion already existed then.

When someone rejects God, God's biblical truth, they become mentally delusional, living in a fictitious matrix. But what about Christian, why would the strong delusion affect them? God reveals through the scriptures to those who love Him, (1 Cor 2:9)", and "those who seek him (Heb 11: 6)." The majority have received the fundamental truth to attain salvation, that suffices, but for many everything else is seen as a metaphor.

Today's technology is a form of magic. In ancient Egypt, magic was proof of their god's appointed authority. Magicians act as an envoy of higher authority to serve Pharoah. Pharaoh magicians carry out many acts of unexplainable phenomenon. They were Pharaoh's wise men and sorcerers, (Exodus 7:11). They copied many of Moses' and Aaron's miracles. Moses and Aaron were God's envoys and magicians in the eyes of the Pharaoh. This was a contest of the supernatural power between God's miracles (Aaron and Moses) and the Pharaoh's magicians empowered by demons. It was done to prove the authority behind the magic. Eventually, Pharaoh's magicians could no longer replicate God's acts with their magic. Pharaoh's magicians admitted that it was Moses God who had greater authority over the supernatural, (Exodus 7:18).

Author's note

What follows will be a shock for many. In 2015, I came across this truth that I am about to share with you. I was very sceptical therefore I left it on the back burner. Eventually, my curiosity got the best out of me and I pursue researching the subject matter. I am not expecting to convince you on the first reading but rather to stirred up your curiosity so that you would further explore the evidence.

God created the heavens and the earth, the sun, moon, and stars with all their constellations as signs of the season found between the water above and the water below. The earth is a circular flat surface with enormous ice ridges as boundaries. The earth is immovable and still. The sun and the moon circle at approximately three thousand miles above the surface of the waters and earth. The sun and the moon are approximately thirty miles in diameter, both creating their own light. The North Star, named Polaris, is fixed in the firmament.

The delusion God created is an impression that the sunrise at dawn and sunset in the evening is made as if the earth is rotating when actually the sun is moving further and further away on the surface of the earth in the evening and coming closer and closer in the morning. God also creates the false impression that the moon reflects the sun, but it is not since there is no shadow view behind the crescent moon, but in daylight, we see the blue sky. A 1965 a scientist claims the moon is plasma, 4 years before the moon landing[75].

The Polaris is fixed above in the sky, proving that the earth does not move either but rather the stars are rotating around the Polaris. If the Polaris were not fixed, how could seaman navigate on the ocean without losing their direction? Why did God create a strong delusion? *"Because they did not receive the love of the truth, that they might be saved."*

Inasmuch as God allowed Pharaoh's magicians to use their power to deceive for the purpose to subdue and bring under control the population, so does God allow Satan to use this delusion to deceive many. Christians fell for Satan's lies, his deceptions and his perspectives of the universe. As in the days of Nebuchadnezzar king of Babylon, there were many astrologers who charted the position of the stars in the sky to gain insight into human personality and even draw predictions about the future, (Daniel 2:2). Astrologers were instruments of Satan to deceive for the purpose to push people away from God. An astrologer is also deceived and manipulated by demons who desire to be worshiped. They love to brag. Astronomers on the other hand usually fall under two main types: either observational or theoretical.

Deceit out of God's Creation – The Calendar

Modern-day astronomers deceive by creating an illusion out of God's creation. They created the 12-month cycle instead of a more dependable 13-month instituted by God to the Jews. Astrology and astronomy are very lucrative. The modern Romanist gives unlimited financial funds and resources to further the cause of this deception. It is arrogant that they claim that the earth does not rotate exactly 24 hrs. What

---

[75] https://youtu.be/XhIwZuPGfss

came first, the creation made by God or their man-made atomic clock?

Taken from https://calendartruth.info/calendar-history/ web site[76], Calendar reform is NOT a new crazy idea

It is important for us to remember that during the first half of the 20th century, a vigorous and well-organized calendar reform movement flourished. George Eastman of Eastman Kodak organized a great campaign on behalf of a particular 13-month, 28-day calendar, known as The International Fixed Calendar, a perpetual calendar (same every year) with 13 equal months of exactly 4 weeks (28 days) each, comprising 364 days, and with the final 365th day held not in any week or month, often known as a "Null Day" or "Zero Day," so that the first day of the year is always the first day of the week, a Sunday.

> In the United States alone, over one hundred industries adopted a 13-month, 28-day perpetual calendar. Kodak used one until 1989. It was announced that on January 1, 1933, we would return to 13 months of 28 days each. But the Vatican resisted it by focusing on a campaign against the "Null Day."
>
> They argued that a break in the succession of the seven-day week would create chaos and calamity. George Eastman Kodak, one of the most well-known 13-month, 28-day calendar proponents of that time, was murdered within the next year after the Vatican stopped the calendar change. This calendar story has been swept under the history carpet. (End of article)

---

[76] https://calendartruth.info/calendar-history/

What is the greatest benefit in hiding the 13-month calendar?

It hides God as the creator of the heavens and the earth. It is God that re-instituted a seven-day week and the 13-month calendar. God used manna to train the Israelites to observe the 7 days' rest, (Exodus 16:27). The 13-month calendar correlated to the Jewish festival. These festivals reveal God prophetic plan of salvation and the establishment of His kingdom on earth. Now that is a good reason to hide the truth, is not?

An important factor is that it creates disharmony with the creation timeline. It causes a disruption in the flow of consciousness; it is like a glitch in the operating system. It causes error and confusion. And this occurs every day for millions of people.

Government and private industries steal from the population billions of dollars in pension and social service payout. Civil servants end up losing 11 days payment from their salary when based on solar Gregorian calendar rather than the Jewish lunar calendar.

Are we so gullible? Are we just going to put the lies and the deceptions under our pillow and sleep on them? This disdainful Romanist NASA organization has the audacity to change God's law of science into lies, for one purpose and that is to push people away from God, to prove that God as the Creator does not exist. They are sons of disobedience, sun worshipers, and Luciferians who venerate Satan, and for some believe that they are from the seed of Cain.

We Christians represent the salt of the earth, the lamp on a lampstand - the truth. Christians have allowed NASA to shove the truth under the rug. NASA "... *having a form of godliness but denying its power. And such people turn away!*" (2 Tim 3:5).

In Ancient Egypt, the origin behind the supernatural phenomenon was without doubt the spirits of the dark world. It was part of politics and religion combined. As it was also in Babylon, so it is today in every nation. Excerpt from a book title, "A History of Israel" by Davis • Whitcomb

> "The Babylonians were indeed fascinated by astronomy signs, for their national life revolved around the movement of the planets and comets against the background of fixed stars and the predicted time intervals of solar and lunar eclipses. Expert "stargazers' ' (called "soothsayers' ' in Dan 2:27) spent their lives taking amazingly accurate astronomy measurements in order to control the superstitious population through astrology. Isaiah challenged these men to save Babylon from divine judgment if they could: *"let now the astrologers, the stargazers, the monthly prognosticators, stand up, and save thee from the things that shall come upon thee"* (Isaiah 47:13). Because of these Babylonian astrologers, millions of heathens were "dismayed at the signs of heaven" (Jer 10:2), and we must admit with sorrow that similar influence is gaining momentum even in so-called Christian America today."

Isn't what NASA does, by amazing the world with deceptive images of the universe to support the theory of the expansion of the universe when the Bible specifically teaches that the stars in the firmament, are below the water above? Inasmuch as the Pharaoh's magicians used their magic to persuade the mass population of the authority of their gods, so did God use supernatural power to persuade the Israelites of His authority, and He did so all through the history of Israel, and the most incredible miracle was moving the shadow backward by ten steps (or degree) at the request of King Hezekiah, (2 Kings 20:10). Jesus performed miracles through the power of the Holy Spirit, although He was accused of using the power of Beelzebub, the ruler of the demons, (Matt 12:24). Can you believe the arrogance of the Sadducees and of the Pharisees? If Pharaoh's magicians would have witnessed Jesus' miracles, they would have admitted that Jesus' power was from God, and they would have perhaps received salvation. The Sadducees and the Pharisees instead, harden their hearts as much as Pharaoh did.

Nowadays scientists through technology act as elitist magicians. There are scientists who serve the true God and there are scientists who serve Satan. Yet there are scientists who know the truth but for the fear of losing their funds, their grants from the government and from NASA prefer to accept the lies. A far contrast from Daniel's three friends, they did not bow to the lies of King Nebuchadnezzar's gold image represents more than a false god; it stands erected representing lies.

Shadrach, Meshach, and Abed-Nego did not fall down on their knees to worship the gold image that King Nebuchadnezzar erected, (Daniel 3:12). There were many Jews attending the ceremonies in which all bowed to the golden image. Yet, Shadrach, Meshach, and Abed-Nego did not fall on their knees to worship the gold image. Most interesting is that they did not protest and tried to rally every Jew attending not to worship the gold image. No, instead, they set an example by allowing the king's servants to toss them alive into a scorching furnace. They set an example of not bowing to the lie. Please read this commentary titled, "They Traded The Truth Of God For Lies."[77]

---

[77] https://www.simplicityinthegospel.com/2015/05/they-traded-truth-of-god-for-lies.html

How many reformers followed the same example of Shadrach, Meshach, and Abed-Nego, by not submitting to the lies but instead chose to be burned on a stake.

There are many flat-earthers on social media who are spreading the truth at their own peril. They are a mix of Christians and seculars. There is a pastor, a defender of flat earth behind the pulpit and outside of his church whose name is Dean Odle running as governor for the state of Alabama.[78] There are many scholars in theology, eschatology, and who hold a Doctorate in Greek and Hebrew proclaiming the inerrancy of the word of God yet would deny Gen 1:6 by explaining that the canopy disperses at the great flood and are embracing the pseudo-scientific explanation that this canopy would have produced a worldwide greenhouse effect resulting in a mild climate throughout the earth. In addition, this canopy would shield man from harmful radiation which influences the aging process. At the great Flood, this canopy collapsed and no longer protect man and the animals... really? It is God that decrees the longevity of man, not pseudoscience, (Psalm 90:10).

Modern Technology is Magic

The mass population does not know how a television set works, how a cell phone works, and how radio frequency goes through the air. Since the population assumed that the scientific community created all these marvels of technology, the population put their trust behind the magic of technology. As it was in ancient times when magicians influenced the population, it is today's technology that controls

---

[78] https://www.deanodleforgovernor.com/

the masses. Magic attracts a crowd, and so do televisions, computers, Xboxes, and I-pads. Technology can easily create strong delusions. A theory is a theory until proven otherwise. NASA and the scientific community use high technology techniques with high-resolution graphics animation (CGI) to influence the mass population to accept their lies as facts. I marvel that they lost the technology to land on the moon. What is the real reason we have not been back to the moon? The hoax of landing on the moon was successful. Everyone on earth fell for the lies. Watch: Elon Musk: it's totally weird we haven't been back to the moon.[79] There are no space satellites orbiting the earth since there is no vacuum space, it is all balloon satellite.[80] Metal balloon satellites filled with helium are permanently on orbit which make it possible to see with our eyes.

Intense undersea communication cables are use from one continent to another. They are also described as the "world's information super-highways, undersea cables carry over 95 percent of international data. In **comparison with satellites**, subsea cables provide high capacity, cost-effective, and reliable connections that are critical for our daily lives. There are approximately more than four hundred active cables worldwide covering 1.3 million kilometers (half a million miles)"[81].

Science fiction movies about space travel such as Star Trek, and Star Wars, and ET Go Home give us the impression that we are not alone in the universe, and acceptance of aliens visiting earth. These movies and TV series are under the category of Pseudoscience. That is why it is called Sci-fi yet perceived as a great possibility. Wikipedia defines science

---

[79] https://youtu.be/ecJBvPYTAeo
[80] https://history.nasa.gov/conghand/ballsat.htm
[81] https://www.csis.org/analysis/invisible-and-vital-undersea-cables-and-transatlantic-security

fiction as a genre of speculative fiction that has been called the "literature of ideas". It typically deals with imaginative and futuristic concepts such as advanced science and technology..., yet Sci-fi is used to deceive people, to turn people away from God.

Many skeptics will ask why God does not demonstrate His presence through supernatural power as He did in the past. That is because the past has proven that many chose not to accept the signs as coming from God the Creator. The Church era is unique in history where believers are to trust God in His word only, by faith alone, (Romans 1:17).

> *"Then the Lord said to Moses: "How long will these people reject Me? And how long will they not believe Me, with all the signs which I have performed among them?"*
> Numbers 14:11.

Were you aware that the word Internet is meant for 'enter my net' as in a trap and the word, Worldwide Web refers to a 'spider web' which is also a trap, and the word Television is perceive as 'tell a vision' as a false perception, which broadcasts a full spectrum of subliminal messages. In the 1970s, the US Federal Communications Commission (FCC) banned the use of subliminal messages in advertisements but are exempt in program shows, movies and within the music industries...hmm, go figure.

In the news media, there is a great emphasis on giving the latest INFORMATION which is meant to keep us "in formation" with the same narrative on each TV stations. We are swimming in a pool of lies. The Church desperately needs discernment.

> *"Folly is joy to him who is destitute of discernment, but a man of understanding walks uprightly,"* Proverbs 15:21

True Christian believers should know that all things have been created by God as written in the Book of Genesis.

> *"By faith we understand that the worlds were framed by the word of God, so that the things which are seen were not made of things which are visible,"* Hebrews 11:3.

"The Proof is in the Pudding " "In the Eating of God's Words"

"The proof, the evidence of God existence is in Genesis 1:6, the blue sky above is water – the earth is in a dome and is flat."

Message to Pastors and Ministers

I have seen and heard many ministers and pastors who took a harsh stand against flat earthers, and against members of their own congregation, to those who literally view Genesis 1:6 true.

Pastors, please to not make a bold statement behind the pulpit not to bring up the flat earth, especially from pastors who claim to believe in the inerrancy of the word of God. You teach to search <u>all the Scriptures</u> .

> *"These were more fair-minded than those in Thessalonica, in that they received the word with all readiness, and searched the Scriptures daily to find out whether these things were so,"* Acts 17:11

One pastor state that "The scripture is like a chain, relating everything to the word of God, one link of that chain miss, broken or taken away would do away with the entire validity, the veracity of the scripture, therefore it cannot be broken," followed by admitting that he does not understanding everything. I love his honesty.

Why would some pastors be so harsh on those after making research that has proven to their curiosity that the earth is flat?

The Pharisees were arrogant to believe to be the keeper of the scripture, as some today and accusing anyone as heresy who view the blue sky as water.

> *"A proud and haughty man— "Scoffer" is his name; He acts with arrogant pride,"* Proverbs 21:24

I give thanks to God for He is good, He who alone does great work, His kindness shall always endure His mercy never fails. I was born in an ocean of lies. I cried out to Him to show me the truth, and He heard my cry.

> *"For the Lord is good; His mercy is everlasting, And His truth endures to all generations,"* Psalm 100:5

Some marvel at Nasa's James Webb Space Telescope, a space telescope designed primarily to conduct infrared astronomy. As the largest optical telescope in space, its high infrared resolution and sensitivity allow it to view objects light years in distant, or faint for the Hubble Space Telescope. They marvel at the clarity of images taken by this telescope of detailed observations of the distant universe. They give praise to God for being the creator of this vast universe not realizing that these images are CGI (computer-generated imagery). Nasa deny this fact. Nasa states that it is creating composite image or picture. A composite result from combining more than one photographic element from various sources in a single picture. The intention is to create a picture (or graphic) where all the elements appear as complementary parts of the same scene[82].

Taken from the https://www.eclipseaviation.com/ web site, this question was asked.[83]

Why Are There No Real Pictures Of Space?

It is important to remember that these images don't constitute a fake image. These are just interpretations of reality according to the scientists who took them up to space. Its real form comes from the real universe; its information is based on fact. To approximate their real colors, scientists create multiple filter photos and paste them together into one image.

> "If you tell a big enough lie and tell it frequently enough, people will eventually come to believe it"
> Adolf Hitler

This quote is true and supported with big money. Billions if not trillions are spent to make God disappear. God is limited and restricted within a spiritual sphere of existence according to personal belief and opinion.

In the churches, the widespread belief is that God is all powerful which is true, therefore, to believe that He created the heavens and the earth with an infinite universe with infinite numbers of galaxies, and stars is an easy notion to accept as

---

[82] https://www.photokonnexion.com/composite-image-definition/

[83] https://www.eclipseaviation.com/why-does-nasa-have-cgi-earth-pictures/

truth. But is it? Many will declare that they are not limiting God power in a box. What does the Bible have to say? Isn't His WORD, and words powerful witness as true?

> *"Hath in these last days spoken unto us by his Son, whom he hath appointed heir of all things, **by whom also he made the worlds;** Who being the brightness of his glory, and the express image of his person, and **upholding all things by the word of his power**, when he had by himself purged our sins, sat down on the right hand of the Majesty on high,"* Heb 1:2-3 KJV

The word of his power; is it not indicative that His word is powerfully true? God does exactly what He said He would do. No more, no less. Again, who are you going to believe? Pseudo-science or the power of God's word? Genesis 1, verse 6, Then God said,

> *"Let there be a firmament in the midst of the waters, and let it divide the waters from the waters."* verse 7 T*hus God made the firmament and divided the waters which were under the firmament from the waters which were above the firmament; and it was so.* Verse 8 *And God called the firmament Heaven.*

The strong Concordance defines Heaven (H8o64) as aloft; the dual perhaps alluding to the visible arch in which the clouds move, as well as to the higher ether where the celestial bodies revolve. A visible arch, a dome like form, and blue in colour…hmmm. Sure looks like water to me. Isn't it? I am not limiting God's power, aux contraire, I agree with the power of His word.

Once the water has been separated, then what?

Verse 16 "Then God made two great lights: the greater light to rule the day, and the lesser light to rule the night. He made the stars also." Verse 17 **God set them IN the firmament of the heavens to give light on the earth,**

The power in the word describes the location of the sun, the moon, and the stars to be IN the firmament, within a dome. The scripture does not limit God's power, it describes exactly the truth about His creation.

Do your research? Use your eyes, and God's gift of discernment. Try to prove the earth is a sphere without Nasa imagery. But most of all, please do not belittle anyone who thinks differently than you without first studying it.

I will never cease to learn from God. (1 Thess 5:21), *"Test all things; hold fast what is good."* and most of all do not turn away anyone who comes to your church and declares to you that he came to believe in God's existence through Flat Earth and wants to know more about how to be saved.

It will happen. Many will come. Be ready for it. Flat earth is the truth that was kept hidden and secret so that so many perished. We all desire and pray for a revival. This desired revival will not come unless we reveal the truth about the shape of the earth and expose the lies. Is it not what the past reformers did concerning the doctrine of salvation, by exposing the lies?

Why was it so important for the Canadian government to make The Charter of Rights and Freedoms powerless for the population during the Covid-19 mandates? It was to take away the power of the Church to defend God's creation. It is a Christian's right to live by a set of beliefs. If a Christian wants to believe that Jesus resurrected which goes against all scientific evidence, it is his/her right to do so and The Charter of Rights and Freedoms will protect his/her belief. If a

Christian wants to believe that the blue sky above is water as described in Genesis 1:6, which does not go against all scientific evidence, it is his/her right to do so and The Charter of Rights and Freedoms will protect his/her belief, and in this case, it is the truth.

The Charter of Rights and Freedoms has not been legislated to protect scientific evidence or unscientific speculation (pseudoscience) such as the theory of evolution or of the big bang theory but the evidence of the written word of God. It is by faith that we understand, and it is by the scriptures that God reveals Himself. The Charter of Rights and Freedoms is not a privilege. The Charter of Rights and Freedoms is a constitution, which is the supreme law in Canada. Christian parents have the right to demand the removal of sex education from the school curriculum that goes against their moral values.

Instead of defending and challenging the government our right to protect our children from moral value that do not reflect Christians values, we pull our children from the school system for home school instead. What victory do we have in compromising? We still pay the school tax. The school board win since parent does not take a stand and if they do, they are alone. The churches be active supporting the parent and of defending the children.

Christian parents have the right to demand not to have their children involve in other religions within the school curriculum, which goes against their spiritual belief that there is only One True God. Christian parents have the right to reclaim the right and parental sovereignty to be the sole teachers of moral and ethical values to their children and the Charter of Rights and Freedoms will defend their rights. No government from any level has any right and responsibility to educate their ideology of belief, (better known as idiotology) moral values and woke principality to any children. Demand from your government to respect your choice of not having sex education and other religion and fairy tale to be taught to your children. It is not their business. The church should establish private school and be eligible to receive school tax. That goes for all nationality and culture. Again, I repeat,

> "True and pure diversity in a multicultural society is to allow each parent to teach their children their religious belief, their values according to their culture and tradition, and to teach their sexual moral standard and behaviour without prejudice and without interference from any level of government. Isn't that what the Charter of Rights and Freedoms is all about?"

Admonition to the Modern Era of the Western Laodicean Nation Churches

God gave us at birth the freedom of conscience, the freedom to come to our own conclusion. Yet, we are so gullible. No wonder Jesus describes us as sheep in need of a good Shepherd. We tend to fall for any deceptions without questioning. Before Adams disobedience by eating the forbitten fruits of the tree of knowledge of good and evil, Adam and Eve were protected by the presence of God. In God's absence, they fell for Satan's lies, his deceptions, and we for Satan's deceptive perspectives of the universe. The Church benefits from the same protection against Satan's lies. We are protected by God's presence that are found in His word, and more, by the presence of the Holy Spirit in us, (bonus).

> *"As for God, His way is perfect; The word of the Lord is proven; He is a shield to **all** who trust in Him,"* 2 Samuel 22:31, Psalm 18:30

> *"Draw near to God and He will draw near to you. Cleanse your hands, you sinners; and purify your hearts, you double-minded,"* James 4:8

> *"Fight the good fight of faith, lay hold on eternal life, to which you were also called and have confessed the good confession in the presence of many witnesses,"* 1 Tim 6:12

The Americans are living a revival in the truth, they seek the truth. They witness the lies generated by these self-proclaimed elites in which bring to ruin their great nation. They recognize that they were responsible of making the wrong choice of staying out of politics. After all, they believed the lies to keep religion and state separated[84]. We know now that Christianity was the target. Please, please stop listening to the mainstream media. Remember, I previously mentioned that the Canadian media have received millions of so call bailout money so that government would keep controlling the narrative of fear. To be in the truth we must stay away from the influence of lies.

> *"You shall not bear false witness against your neighbor,"* Exodus 20:16

To the Canadian Laodiceans, we have lost our rights and freedoms. Nothing is back to normal, and you know it. We are helpless, like sheep to the slaughter. The last blow to bring you to submission is coming soon. Do not be like the German Jews who refused to see all the signs which warned them to get out of Germany. This time all Canadian citizens are targeted. Only those who submit to the lies and conform to the cult of this New World in disorder will be temporarily

---

[84] https://youtu.be/7v-G66jbyuE

spared from the concentration camps called isolation facilities. Many have started to succumb to the adverse effect of the vaccine and some to their death. As of November 18, 2022, according to Dr. William Makis, there are 93 dead doctors after vaccine rollout in Canada[85]. If 93 doctors died so far, how many more in the Canadian population died due to the vaccine? The media is silence. What narrative will the media use to cover up. There is a sudden death tsunami is happening right now[86]. Who are they going to blame? The Ontario College of Physicians and Surgeons sent a memo to all the Ontario doctors suggesting considering diagnostic their unvaccinated patience with mental problem. mental problem[87].

There is nothing new under the sun. Niro, the Roman Caesar, willfully ordered the burning of Rome and blamed the Christians to fulfill his project of a new Rome. The Romanists still are in power under a new name and there is nothing standing in their way for the New World in-disorder, except the Church. You might view that all faith, all culture, and tradition are under attack. Make no mistake, the Romanists are after Christians only, since we are the resistance, the Holy Spirit that reside in the Church.

Isn't it time to turn to Our Lord?

"But as for me, I trust in You, O Lord;
I say, "You are my God."
My times are in Your hand;
Deliver me from the hand of my enemies,

---

[85] https://rumble.com/embed/v1spu0s/?pub=gi6jj

[86] https://rumble.com/v1vzv3q-died-suddenly-the-safe-and-effective-compilation.html

[87] https://rumble.com/embed/v1spu0s/?pub=gi6jj

And from those who persecute me,"
Psalm 31:14-15
"Restore us, O God of our salvation,
And cause Your anger toward us to cease.
Will You be angry with us forever?
Will You prolong Your anger to all generations?
Will, You not revive us again,
That Your people may rejoice in You?
Show us Your mercy, Lord,
And grant us Your <u>salvation,</u>" (preservation and deliverance from harm, ruin)
Psalm 85:4-7

In Psalm 86, David prayed for Mercy, with Meditation on the Excellencies of the Lord

Canadian Christians let personalize this prayer as a group who implores God Divine intervention in our lives and our nation.

1   *Bow down Your ear, O Lord, hear (us);*
    For (we are) poor and needy.
2   *Preserve (our lives), for (we are) holy;*
    You are (our) God;
    Save Your servant(s) who trusts in You!
3   *Be merciful to (us), O Lord,*
    For (we) cry to You all day long.
4   *Rejoice the soul of Your servant(s),*
    For to You, O Lord, (we) lift up (our souls).
5   *For You, Lord, are good, and ready to forgive,*
    And abundant in mercy to all those who call upon You.
6   *Give ear, O Lord, to (our) prayer(s);*
    And attend to the voice of (our) supplications.
7   *In the day of (our) trouble (we) will call upon You,*

	For You will answer (us).
8	*Among the gods there is none like You, O Lord;*
	Nor are there any works like Your works.
9	*All nations whom You have made*
	Shall come and worship before You, O Lord,
	And shall glorify Your name.
10	*For You are great, and do wondrous things;*
	You alone are God.
11	*Teach (us) Your way, O Lord;*
	(We) will walk in Your truth;
	Unite (our) heart(s) to fear Your name.
12	*(We) will praise You, O Lord (our) God, with all (our) heart,*
	And (we) will glorify Your name forevermore.
13	*For great is Your mercy toward (us),*
	And You have delivered (our) soul(s) from the depths of Sheol.
14	*O God, the proud have risen against (us),*
	And a mob of violent men have sought (our lives),
	And have not set You before them.
15	*But You, O Lord, are a God full of compassion, and gracious,*
	Longsuffering and abundant in mercy and truth.
16	*Oh, turn to (us), and have mercy on (us)!*
	Give Your strength to Your servant(s),
	And save the sons of Your maidservant(s).
17	*Show (us) a sign for good,*
	That those who hate (us) may see it and be ashamed,
	Because You, Lord, have helped (us) and comforted (us).

Verse 17 request a sign for good, a demonstration, evidence of God's present in our lives and a symbol to our enemies. This sign for good is God's creation, the blue sky above is water just as describes in Genesis 1:6.

The Greatest Revival is Starting Now with You.

Answer the knocking at the door.

> *"Behold, I stand at the door and knock. If anyone hears My voice and opens the door, I will come in to him and dine with him, and he with Me,"* Revelation 3:20

But how do I do that, you ask? The knocking at the door literally happen to me over fifty years ago when a door- to door salesman knock at my door. That is when I invited Jesus to come and dine with me, by the purchase of His words the bible. How would I had known then that He was preparing me for this dark time in our nation. Who me? Yes, I who had many failures in my life. Believe me when I tell you that it is all God's doing in the writing of this book. God is proving to the proud elites of this world that He use anyone He chose to, even the most insignificant as I am.

The knocking at the door is your calling to stewardship. Surely the Holy Spirit is stirring up the will and the desires in your heart, (Col 1:9). Do not quench the Spirit, (1Thess 5:19). Give your all to Jesus, your time, your treasures, and your talents. As little are your treasures and may be your talents, God will multiply them, (John 21:13). You will not be alone. He will be dining with you. Night and day He will be with you, you will be regarded as a friend, a great friend. I have tears coming in my eyes just thinking of that part. You have no idea what the fruit of your effort will be, as small as it could be. Remember the feeding the five thousand in (Matt 14:13.)

> *"For who hath despised the day of small things? for they shall rejoice, and shall see the plummet in the hand of Zerubbabel with those seven; they are the eyes of the Lord, which run to and fro through the whole earth,"*
> Zechariah 4:10 KJV (read the whole chapter)

Nehemiah representing God's people who wanted to continuously be bless in the reconstruction of Jerusalem's walls and the Temple, (Neh 5:19, 13:14,22,31). It started with a small group of Jews returning from 70 years of captivity from Babylon while other Jews stayed behind for the wealthy comfortable living. This small group faced humongous challenges such as persecution, assassination attempt, hunger, and discouragement. They were poor and needy of all sorts of supplies. Was it worst, they asked? The wealthy have the most to lose and harder to let it go. As it was for the young rich man in (Mark 10:17-22), is it also hard for the corporate church and some members to let go of the Tax-exemption status which restricts them from being an active partisan in the great revival. It is inevitable the Tax-exemption will be taken away.

It will take as much sacrifice from our part to build a revival in our land as it took for the Israelites to rebuild the wall and the Temple. Only a very few will accept the call by answering the door. Will the revival be responsible for the preparation of the 144,000 of all the tribes of the children of Israel to minister to the entire world, (Revelation 7:4)? The Bible does not reveal it. Will the fruit of the revival be responsible for a great multitude which no one could number, of all nations, tribes, peoples, and tongues, standing before the throne and before the Lamb, clothed with white robes, with palm branches in their hands, that come out of the great tribulation, and washed their robes and made them white in the blood of the Lamb for not taking the mark of the beast and of not genuflected before the beast, (Rev 7:9,14)? The Bible does not reveal it.

What the bible revealed is that to whoever open the door will be reward with a reward that surpasses all previous rewards. In the Bible, the rewards for the believers are identified with five crowns in total:

- the Everlasting Crown (Victory) (1 Cor 9:24-27) - overcoming man's sinful nature through our Lord Jesus
- the Crown of the Soul Winner (Phil 4:1 and 1 Thess 2:19-20) - reaching out - sharing the gospel (Matt 28:19)
- the Crown of Righteousness (2 Tim 4:8) - longing for Jesus' return
- the Crown of Life (James 1:12, Rev 2:10) - enduring through trials
- the Crown of Glory (1 Peter 5:4) - ministering to God's people

These crowns are presented to us at the Bema Seat which immediately followed the return of our Redeemer for the saints known as an event called the rapture. The reward that surpasses all crowns is not a crown, but a position of authority.

> *"To him who overcomes I will grant to sit with Me on My throne, as I also overcame and sat down with My Father on His throne,"* Revelation 3:21

That seat at the right side of Jesus was a subject of dispute among the disciples, remember?

> *"So Jesus said to them, "You will indeed drink the cup that I drink, and with the baptism I am baptized with you will be baptized; but to sit on My right hand and on*

> *My left is not Mine to give, <u>but it is for those for whom it is prepared</u>,"* Mark 10:39-40

Do not wait wither or not you have your house in order as admonish in (1 Timothy 3:2-4). The only requirement is to open the door and to let Jesus take over your life no matter what the circumstance and condition you find yourself in. Let Jesus transforms your heart. Once the hearts have been translated, then we get to work shooting "LAST CALL," blowing the trumpet, some as prophets to the kings and leaders of the world, (Rev10:11) some to share the gospel and some as shepherds and teachers to unite the churches. (Eph 4: 11-13).

For those who refuse to answer the door, to open it, to let our Lord Jesus enter, you have received a fair warning. You now know too much to stay idle. Bottom line there is one thing you can do, PRAY, PRAY, PRAY for God to keep on knocking as many doors as possible worldwide and especially in our nation Canada, to stir up the heart to answer the door.

> *"But he who did not know yet committed things deserving of stripes shall be beaten with few. For everyone to whom much is given, from him much will be required, and to whom much has been committed, of him, they will ask the more,"* Luke 12:48

Conclusion

Today, our freedoms and parental sovereignty over our children have been taken away because we took civil liberty for granted. We let this freedom go astray to a point where many take this liberty to sin evermore. As I previously mentioned, who would die for a sinful nation that pollutes the mind of our Christian and non-Christian children's minds by teaching the woke ideology and lifestyle behaviour in our school that goes against the parents? Who would die for a sinful nation that allows murdering unborn babies for the sake of convenience? Who would die for the leaders of a country who chose to serve the interest of The United Nations, the House of Rothschild, the Cabal, selling out the sovereignty of our national economy - for the creation of a New Word in Dis-order? WHO?

Jesus would… He already did.

Defend first your parental sovereignty over our children. Challenge them in all levels of government. That is your priority.

> *"He will bring justice to the poor of the people; He will save the children of the needy,*
> *And will break in pieces the oppressor,"*
> Psalm 72:4

> *"Greater love has no one than this, than to lay down one's life for his ~~friends~~, children"*
> John 15:13

Final Word

The earth is flat, and the moon landing was produced in a studio. If you fall for the fraud of the moon landing, you are not alone, including myself and billions of people around the world. The moon landing hoax was aired on July 20, 1969, I was 16 years old and a fan of Star Trek which was first broadcast on September 6, 1966, on Canada's CTV network. My generation were already indoctrinated to accept any hoax, after all we grow up with an earth globe in the classroom. If I and so many millions of people fall for the fraud of the moon landing, we are vulnerable to fall for any hoax, especially if the hoax is created by imagination. I came across a well-done presentation on the origin of the globe earth. Please watch it. Title, "Helios sorcery | Exposing the Occult Origins of Heliocentrism" https://rumble.com/embed/v1tuh76/?pub=gi6jj

As so many now recognize that the fear of the Covid-19 virus has become more dangerous than the virus itself. That was the narrative broadcast in all major mainstream media, fear. According to the statistic provide by Justice Centre for Constitutional Freedoms the mortality rate was no greater than 0.05% of the population. The population of the age of 80 years old and over were among the group with the most death rate[88]. According to the Ottawa Public Health a total of 840 Ottawa residents have died of COVID-19 since March 2020. The majority of deaths are in people over the age of 60. Ottawa population in 2022 is 944,753, therefore the percentage death by covid-19 per population in the last two years is 0.09% percent, which comes to 0.044% per

---

[88] https://www.jccf.ca/covid-stats/

years. This is far, far from being considered as a pandemic. It is no more serious than the flu.

Yet the media keeps pushing the narrative of fear. Fear is a deep feeling of uncertainty and insecurity that could easily turn into panic. Panic creates a loss of composure, a loss of self-possession to think rationally, a quality of being guided by or based on reason. Many Canadians, as well as many around the world submitted to the guidance of the government directive motivated by fear alone. Many who have a sense of rationality succumbed to the fear of losing their job if they did not submit to the government mandate. Few Canadians had the courage to live according to their conviction and disobeyed the government mandate and restriction by not taking the vaccine, consequently lost their jobs.

About me

When the time came, I decided not to take the jab, in which my wife totally supported the decision. I was the only bread winner of the household. Two years prior to the hoax of Covid-19 I was retired and settled in a small town in Newfoundland and Labrador. One of my daughters living in Ottawa had health issues, a single parent of three children, the youngest a baby. My wife and I moved to Ottawa and rented an apartment across from my daughter apartment. My wife easily found a job. I found a position as a security guard. I eventually found employment as an IT service desk agent, on a contract with the federal government.

My wife after a year of service with the company was laid off. She took this opportunity to take a college course in executive business administration. At the same period of time my sister required my assistance with my mother's need at an old age resident in Montreal. The staff were interfering with the well-being of my mother. My mother of 99 years was suffering from severe arthritis and required special needs that the care giver would not provide. A hidden camera witnesses neglect, it was reported and instead of resolving the issues the residence sanction my sister from being giving assistance to my mother. That is when I got involved by being by my mother's side. We hired a lawyer to reinstate the right to my sister to be present at my mother side. But it came with conditions. She was only allowed to be present from 11 am to 9 pm. At that period, my mother's health started to deteriorate also, so I took the night shift while my sister took the dayshift to look after my mother. Eventually the restriction was removed completely but we continued to keep our shift.

My mother passed away with my brother and my sister at her side. Her passing away happened one week before the mandatory lockdown. My wife succeeded in all her courses with high honours. She was in her coop term when she got involved in an automobile accident. Although she did not require hospitalization she suffered whiplash, a concussion, a neck, and shoulder injury with torn and severed ligaments. She was unable to complete her coop term therefore she was denied her diploma. Expenses accumulated, our debt increased getting harder to manage. On December the 16th, 2021, I was put on leave of absent without pay since I was not vaccinated, even if at that time of my employment, I was working from home. We gave our two months' notice to the property owner and moved in my daughter's basement of who coincidentally moved into a house rental from an apartment rental. As an IT service desk agent, I listened to many government workers who suffered dearly from the lock down. There was one in particularly whose mother was also in need of her as a nanny to look after all her care that the resident care giver did not provide. She was denied access to be with her mother. It got worse in the residence, with the government $400 per week assistance for those who experienced a minor sign of a cold symptom would stay home to cash in, therefore causing a shortage in all residence across Canada.

Her mother's health deteriorated, she was transferred to a hospital, and was denied being at her mother's death bed. She was crying with great sorrow on the phone. I felt the pain in my heart, and I took all the time in the world to comfort her.

There are thousands who suffered during the lock down, many more due to the mandatory vaccine. NOT A WORD WAS MENTIONED IN THE MAINSTREAM MEDIA OF ALL THE SUFFERING. But God heard all the cries, the lamentations, the desperate cry of all mothers and fathers, He seen the desperate acts of suicide among the teenagers.

I am a Christian, not perfect in my faith, in walking with God. I had many moments of doubt and in trusting in God. I was grateful to have the support of my congregation in prayers and encouragement. If you do not belong to a church congregation, find one, a bible believing congregation with the power of God's word as foundation. Find one that teaches the truth. After all Jesus warned us *"For many will come in My name, saying, 'I am the Christ, and will deceive many,"* (Matt 24:5). Judged the word that comes out of their mouths as much as you judge them by their actions. It is important to be connected to the truth, God's truth given through the Holy Spirit to guide us through trouble water of lies and deceptions.

"Jesus said to him, "I am the way, the truth, and the life. No one comes to the Father except through Me," John 14:6

"The Lord is righteous in her midst, He will do no unrighteousness. Every morning He brings His justice to light; He never fails, But the unjust knows no shame," Zephaniah 3:5

Jesus is knocking at your door. Please let Him in and dine with Him for the sake of all the children of the world and for the sake all those who seek His truth.

Epilogue

Covid-19 is a lie, and the globe earth is a lie, both orchestrated by the Romanists. They purposely hide God so that you would never discover that you are created in His image and to be part of His kingdom.

Not all nations failed for the Covid-19 pandemic lie. The nations that did not are Sweden, South Korea, Tajikistan, and the state of Florida, U.S.A. but all nations fail for the lie of globe earth in a heliocentric system, (Rev 18:23).

The truth about the flat earth needs to be disclosed for two reasons. First, it will set us free. Second, a clear choice to accept Jesus as Lord or to reject Him will be offered. What is truth? asked Pontius Pilate to Jesus. Jesus standing in front of him, Pontius Pilate could not tell that Jesus was the way, the truth, and the life. The blue sky above is water. Do not be blinded. As Pontius Pilate witnessed the presence of God in from of him, so are we seeing the truth above our heads? Do your research.

Here are a few links to start with. One is from Pastor Tyler J. Doka using the KJV Bible preaching that flat earth is truth, https://youtu.be/V6yHPRsxyRo

The second one did an excellent presentation series call, "FLAT EARTH Clues by Mark Sargent, https://www.youtube.com/watch?v=T8-YdgU-CF4&index=2&list=PLltxIX4B8_URNUzDE2sXctnUAEXgEDDGn

This one from Earthen Vessels titled, "Helios sorcery | Exposing the Occult Origins of Heliocentrism, https://rumble.com/embed/v1tuh76/?pub=gi6jj

All links that I referred to will eventually be removed by the elites, therefore please share as many as possible and if permitted download them.

The Choice of Life or Death
Deuteronomy 30:11-20

11 For this commandment which I command thee this day, it is not hidden from thee, neither is it far off.

12 It is not in heaven, that thou shouldest say, Who shall go up for us to heaven, and bring it unto us, that we may hear it, and do it?

13 Neither is it beyond the sea, that thou shouldest say, Who shall go over the sea for us, and bring it unto us, that we may hear it, and do it?

14 But the word is very nigh unto thee, in thy mouth, and in thy heart, that thou mayest do it.

15 See, I have set before thee this day life and good, and death and evil;

16 In that I command thee this day to love the Lord thy God, to walk in his ways, and to keep his commandments and his statutes and his judgments, that thou mayest live and multiply: and the Lord thy God shall bless thee in the land whither thou goest to possess it.

17 But if thine heart turn away, so that thou wilt not hear, but shalt be drawn away, and worship other gods, and serve them;

18 I denounce unto you this day, that ye shall surely perish, and that ye shall not prolong your days upon the land, whither thou passest over Jordan to go to possess it.

19 I call heaven and earth to record this day against you, that I have set before you life and death, blessing and cursing: therefore choose life, that both thou and thy seed may live:

20 That thou mayest love the Lord thy God, and that thou mayest obey his voice, and that thou mayest cleave unto him: for he is thy life, and the length of thy days: that thou mayest dwell in the land which the Lord sware unto thy fathers, to Abraham, to Isaac, and to Jacob, to give them.

Let us pray

Father, deliver us from evil
(from the lies, and from the deceptions)

Let thy kingdom comes

Let thy will be done on earth as it is in heaven
Amen

To the left behind

I cannot imagine the overwhelming fear that your mind is going through at the sight of millions of people and children disappearing. Even a child in a woman's womb disappeared, and it is not stillborn. There is no sign of blood. Many of you will quickly realize that this phenomenon called the rapture was predicted but you waited. You waited for the right time in your life to accept Jesus as Lord by faith alone through grace alone. There was a great revival all over the world. There were signs that all things were going to get better. America was doing great again. In Canada, there were victories in the Justice system. The churches were declaring the glory of God, His creation ... preaching the truth. Thousands believed and repented, accepting Jesus as Lord. There was a revival worldwide. But you were skeptical, proud believing that the good time was back to stay.

Now you witness chaos and confusion worldwide. It will take a while before leaders grab hold of the situation, and then the man of sin will be revealed. He will come as a saviour and all nations of the world will submit all their national sovereignty to him. He will rebuild the nations and prosper. He will subdue internal revolts. He will abolish all government's establishment and create new institutions that favoured his aspiration to reign over all the world. He will confirm a covenant with many for one week, an agreement between Israel and surrounding nations, which include the building of a new Temple in Jerusalem. He will name himself god. He will war against those who reject to worship the image of the beast, and who refuse its mark.

In as much as the Romanists were after Christians before the rapture, since they were the resistance through the Holy Spirit that resides in the Church, you have now become the resistance. Your heart will desire to obey our Lord Jesus to the peril of your life. You will receive the blessing for your labour and for the works to uphold the truth, for keeping the commandment of God and the faith of Jesus, (Rev 14: 12-13). An angel will give you hope and courage to resist the beast (Rev 14:6-7) but will not intervene. You will have to work for your salvation, to war to protect one another believers. You will have to resist the beast, not to bow down to the image of the beast, and to reject the mark either on your right hand or on your foreheads, (Rev 13:13, 16). You will be in hiding, pursued, and you will be betrayed by your family. At night, you will look up in heaven and will worship God the creator who made heaven and earth, knowing that His throne is above the dome over the North pole. You will be part of a great multitude which no one could number, of all nations, tribes, peoples, and tongues, standing before the throne and before the Lamb, clothed with white robes, with palm branches in their hands, and crying out with a loud voice, saying, "Salvation belongs to our God who sits on the throne, and to the Lamb!" All the angels stood around the throne and the elders and the four living creatures, and fell on their faces before the throne and worshiped God, saying:

"Amen! Blessing and glory and wisdom,
Thanksgiving and honour and power and might,
Be to our God forever and ever.
Amen." (Rev 7:9-12)

You were described as such by one of an elder who spoke to John,

"These are the ones who come out of the great tribulation and washed their robes and made them white in the blood of the Lamb. Therefore they are before the throne of God and serve Him day and night in His temple. And He who sits on the throne will dwell among them. They shall neither hunger anymore nor thirst anymore; the sun shall not strike them, nor any heat; for the Lamb who is amid the throne will shepherd them and lead them to living fountains of waters. And God will wipe away every tear from their eyes," (Rev 7:14-17).

You are the fruits of the Greatest Revival ever next after Christ's Greatest Revival accomplished by in His resurrection.

Let God Be Magnified

Appendix

A PDF copy of my book titled, "Canadian Christian Ministry 2018 - The Most Lukewarm Church in the whole western nations," is available free on Dropbox

E-Reference available at https://www.simplicityinthegospel.com/p/e-index-greatest-revival.html

Links of all the References mention in this book

Page 6 s. 2(a) https://www.canlii.org/en/ca/laws/stat/schedule-b-to-the-canada-act-1982-uk-1982-c-11/latest/schedule-b-to-the-canada-act-1982-uk-1982-c-11.html#sec2paraa_smooth

Page 6 Charter https://www.canlii.org/en/ca/laws/stat/schedule-b-to-the-canada-act-1982-uk-1982-c-11/latest/schedule-b-to-the-canada-act-1982-uk-1982-c-11.html

Page 7 The Honourable Judge Renee M. Pomerance verdict; https://www.canlii.org/en/on/onsc/doc/2022/2022onsc1344/2022onsc1344.html?searchUrlHash=AAAAAQBKUnVsaW5nIG9uIH-RoZSBDb25zdGl0dXRpb25hbCBWYWxpZGl0eSBvZiBSZWxpdX MgR2F0aGVyaW5nIFJlc3RyaWN0aW9ucyAAAAAAAQ&resultIndex=2

Page 6 Canadian Church sanctuary https://www.jstor.org/stable/48648345?seq=10#metadata_info_tab_contents

Page 7 Conquered by treachery https://www.simplicityinthegospel.com/2022/01/canadas-institutions-conquered.html

Page 8 "Doctor Kelly Victory is explaining everything about covid-19" https://rumble.com/embed/v1pl00m/?pub=gi6jj

Page 9 Agenda 2030 https://en.wikipedia.org/wiki/Sustainable_Development_Goals

Page 9 The Great Reset | COVID-19 BEAST System Explained https://rumble.com/embed/vz59je/?pub=gi6jj

Page 10 James Topp met with MPs in person for over an hour today to have an open conversation. https://rumble.com/v19fpznwatch-james-topp-met-with-mps-in-person-for-over-an-hour-today-to-have-an-o.html

Page 11 Justice Centre for Constitution Freedom
https://www.jccf.ca/justice-centre-files-response-to-feds-request-that-court-throw-out-travel-ban-lawsuit

Page 11 Pastor feeding the homeless https://thefreethoughtproject.com/be-the-change/covid-19-homeless-pastor-fined

Page 11 Pastor arrested for defying covid-19 restriction
https://www.thestar.com/news/canada/2021/02/21/church-whose-pastor-was-arrested-for-defying-covid-19-restrictions-holds-service.html

Page 11 The Great Reset by   Dr. Gene Kim
https://youtu.be/2Xwilhs6Ou8

Page 12 Little Horn Referred to The Anti-Christ"
https://www.simplicityinthegospel.com/2019/05/personality-and-characteristic-of.html

Page 13 Coup D'états & the Plot to Steal America, Canada, and the Western Democracy –
https://rumble.com/embed/vnyykq/?pub=4

Page 13   Lord Mountbatten coup d'état attempt
https://www.historyextra.com/period/20th-century/lord-mountbatten-did-prince-philip-uncle-attempt-lead-coup-harold-wilson-government-crown-true/

Page 16 The Borg of the Start Trek Voyager series sci fi to become reality in fifty years. https://rumble.com/embed/v19n7v9/?pub=gi6jj

Page 17 Canadian Peoples Union website; https://www.thepowershift.ca/about

Page 19   Ottawa Police Officer, Helen Grus   https://canoe.com/news/local-news/suspended-detective-accused-of-seeking-links-between-child-deaths-and-covid-19-vaccines-set-to-return-to-work-lawyer-says-but-ops-says-no-timeline-has-been-set/wcm/a5f2f9d3-1eca-4f4c-8450-44c3631bbff7

Page 19   Alarm sounded on increased incidence of stillborn
https://www.worldtribune.com/alarm-sounded-on-increased-incidence-of-stillborns-reported-among-vaccinated-mothers/

Page 20 No More Lockdowns - https://nomorelockdowns.ca/

Page 20 Dereck Sloan, leader of The Ontario Party https://www.ontarioparty.ca/

Page 20 Sixteen United Conservative Party MLAs https://www.leafythings.com/blog/sixteen-government-mlas-speak-out-against-latest-alberta-public-health-restrictions

Page 20 Independence Party of Alberta https://www.abindependence.com/

Page 22 Police on Guard for Thee, https://policeonguard.ca/whistleblowers/

Page 22 Vaccine Choice Canada https://vaccinechoicecanada.com/

Page 23 THE PLOT https://www.simplicityinthegospel.com/2020/04/the-plot.html

Page 24 News media who secretly took Trudeau's $61M pre-election pay-off https://www.rebelnews.com/exclusive_news_media_who_secretly_took_trudeaus_61m_pre-election_pay-off

Page 24 Which Media Benefited from the Trudeau Government's Covid-19 Funds? https://www.canadaland.com/canadian-media-liberals-trudeau-government-funding-covid-cbc-erin-otoole/

Page 25 Trudeau anti-Christian statement https://www.ipcprayer.org/ipc-connections/item/11834-canada-justin-trudeau-christians-worst-part-of-society.html

Page 27 Canada Has De Facto Political Prisoners https://westandunited.cloud/canada-has-de-facto-political-prisoners/

Page 29 Clip: The Truth About Communism - Jordan Peterson https://youtu.be/VIU8WAFixWs

Page 29 Agenda 21 https://sustainabledevelopment.un.org/outcomedocuments/agenda21/

Page 30 Ontario Party https://www.ontarioparty.ca/

Page 30 Population Control https://thearcanelaboratory.com/watch-bill-gates-admits-to-human-depopulation-program/

Page 32 Double speak – William Lutz, http://www.booknotes.org/Watch/10449-1/William-Lutz

Page 45 The Spirit of Cain https://www.simplicityinthegospel.com/2012/08/spirit-of-cain.html

Page 46 Dispensation https://youtu.be/VnTj--yWydY

Page 47 INTERFAITH - The Gathering of the Tares https://www.simplicityinthegospel.com/2013/05/interfaith-gathering-of-tares.html

Page 44 Repentance Is a Must https://www.simplicityinthegospel.com/2011/07/repentance-is-must.html

Page 48 Christianity is like the menu of an Ice Cream Parlour https://www.simplicityinthegospel.com/2011/01/christianity-is-like-menu-of-ice-cream.html

Page 49 Praying to Dead Saints or loved ones https://www.simplicityinthegospel.com/2009/11/praying-to-dead-saints-or-love-one.html

Page 49 Randy Hillier https://www.randyhilliermpp.com/about

Page 54 Lie, or Lose Your Children https://www.cccc.org/news_blogs/intersection/2018/04/04/lie-or-lose-your-children/

Page 47 Christians - The Guardian of The Charter of Rights and Freedoms https://www.simplicityinthegospel.com/2019/11/christians-stand-on-guard-for-thee.html

Page 51 The Covid Lies https://rumble.com/embed/v113v4n/?pub=gi6jj

Page 52 Nurses not complying with the covid-19 emergency policies, https://www.cbc.ca/news/canada/london/ontario-nurses-pandemic-libel-suit-1.6307238

Page 53 Virology papers out of Wuhan in December 2019 https://rumble.com/vy9mv7-the-viral-delusion-part-1-behind-the-curtain-of-the-pandemic-and-the-pseud.html

Page 56 When Did I Receive the Gift of Eternal Life? https://www.simplicityinthegospel.com/2013/10/when-did-i-receive-gift-of-eternal-life.html

Page 61 'Unknown Cause' Is the Top Cause of Death in Canada! https://www.globalresearch.ca/unknown-cause-top-cause-death-canada/5791610

Page 62 "Trudeau's MAID Euthanasia Program to Allow Doctors To Kill Kids Without Parental Consent - Kid depress because he doesn't have a girlfriend" - https://youtu.be/nX4MURUeLog

Page 61 The unknown causes of death - Dr. Kelly Victory https://rumble.com/embed/v1bl5br/?pub=4

Page 61   Unprecedented Rise in Deaths from 'Unknown Causes' Becomes Leading Killer in 2020 and 2021 https://adversereactionreport.com/reactions/alberta-canada-unprecedented-rise-in-deaths-from-unknown-causes-becomes-leading-killer-in-2020-and-2021/

Page 65   Interfaith - The Great Apostasy https://www.simplicityinthegospel.com/2013/05/interfaith-gathering-of-tares.html

Page 67 The Thief on the Cross (Pastor Charles Lawson) https://youtu.be/OGWLuwTfaXs

Page 67 Where Did Jesus Go for Three Days and Three Nights after He was   Crucified - Hank Lindstrom https://youtu.be/fqXjCv2308E

Page 69 Canada's Institutions Conquered" https://www.simplicityinthegospel.com/2022/01/canadas-institutions-conquered.html

Page 69 Masonic Illuminati: Created and Ruled by the Black Pope and Select High Jesuits https://vaticanassassins.org/2011/12/23/masonic-iluminiati-created-and-ruled-by-the-black-pope-and-select-high-jesuits/

Page 69 Freemasonry https://youtu.be/GrBEy2rzhvk

Page 71   Peter McCullough, MD, MPH expose the danger of the vaccine   https://rumble.com/vnbv86-winning-the-war-against-therapeutic-nihilism-and-trusted-treatments-vs-unte.html

Page 71 Dr. Mike Yeadon report that they Lied About Everything, Including That There Was a Pandemic https://rumble.com/v1qztky-dr.-mike-yeadon-they-lied-about-everything-including-that-there-was-a-pande.html

Page 78 The Pulpit Versus the Government https://youtu.be/iNdvTveD-k8

Page 78 Dean Odle for Governor https://www.youtube.com/channel/UCmh0C-1XAyvthMXQB3wt_Fg

Page 78 How we should we vote (series) Dean Bible Ministries https://www.youtube.com/watch?v=pz2khE8QDTg&list=PL1ZC-1HJaptxZxtaLlcd6lBC9Pfbay4dp

Page 78 The Local Church's Role in Government - Craig Northcott https://youtu.be/_DRZ14A_QYI

Page 78 And We Know Channel https://rumble.com/c/AndWeKnow

Page 78 "The Sevenfold Doctrine of Creation" https://www.youtube.com/playlist?list=PLJdMH7D12j5OoDrVSfd-Oh70wwz0uNnzB

Page 79   Missing Children Database https://missingkids.ca/en/missing-children-database/

Page 79 Trafficking of Children for Prostitution and the UNICEF Response https://asiasociety.org/trafficking-children-prostitution-and-unicef-response

Page 84 Charitable Tax Exemption - A Pact with The Devil https://www.simplicityinthegospel.com/2018/10/charitable-tax-exemption-pack-with-devil.html

Page 87 The untold story of Muammar Gaddafi, https://youtu.be/HjmJHLanY3M

Page 88 Deceptive Ruse - Thesis, Antithesis, Synthesis https://www.simplicityinthegospel.com/2018/12/deceptive-ruse-thesis-antithesis_20.html

Page 91 Canadian Charter of Rights and Freedoms vs The Canadian Human Rights Commission https://www.simplicityinthegospel.com/2019/02/canadian-charter-of-rights-and-freedoms.html

Page 92 Leave us alone or reap the whirlwind - Jordan B. Peterson https://youtu.be/--QS_UyW2SY

Page 92 Peddlers of environmental doom have shown their true totalitarian colours - Jordan B Peterson https://www.telegraph.co.uk/news/2022/08/15/peddlers-environmental-doom-have-shown-true-totalitarian-colours/

Page 95 Have You Traded Your Soul? Is It a Done Deal? https://www.simplicityinthegospel.com/2012/12/have-you-traded-your-soul.html

Page 87 Merry Christmas or Happy Holiday?" https://www.simplicityinthegospel.com/2014/11/merry-christmas-or-happy-holiday.html

Page 100 The Unbelievers https://www.simplicityinthegospel.com/2014/04/john-666.html

Page 103 The Vatican Concordat with Hitler's Reich: The Concordat of 1933 was ambiguous in its day and remains so https://www.americamagazine.org/faith/2003/09/01/vatican-concordat-hitlers-reich-concordat-1933-was-ambiguous-its-day-and-remains

Page 110 United Nations Destroying the U.S.A. by Myron C. Fagan (1967) https://www.bitchute.com/video/JC8MBjJcLxkS/

Page 113 1965 scientist claims the moon is plasma https://youtu.be/XhIwZuPGfss

Page 114 Lunar calendar https://calendartruth.info/calendar-history/

Page 117 They Traded the Truth of God for Lies https://www.simplicityinthegospel.com/2015/05/they-traded-truth-of-god-for-lies.html

Page 118 Dean Odle running as governor for the state of Alabama https://www.deanodleforgovernor.com/

Page 119 Elon Musk: it's totally weird we haven't been back to the moon. https://youtu.be/ecJBvPYTAeo

Page 119 Balloon Satellites https://history.nasa.gov/conghand/ballsat.htm

Page 128 Dr. Andy Woods "The Big Lie" https://youtu.be/7v-G66jbyuE

Page 123 Why Are There No Real Pictures Of Space? https://www.eclipseaviation.com/why-does-nasa-have-cgi-earth-pictures/

Page 123 Definition: Composite image https://www.photokonnexion.com/composite-image-definition/

Page 129 93 Dead Doctors After Vaccine Rollout https://rumble.com/embed/v1spu0s/?pub=gi6jj

Page 129 Died Suddenly: The Safe And Effective Compilation https://rumble.com/v1vzv3q-died-suddenly-the-safe-and-effective-compilation.html

Page 137 Covid-19 statistic https://www.jccf.ca/covid-stats/

"The Great Controversy," by E.G White, ISBN 978-1-629131-72-6.

Page 142 KJV preaching that flat earth, https://youtu.be/V6yHPRsxyRo

Page 142 FLAT EARTH Clues https://www.youtube.com/watch?v=T8-YdgU-CF4&index=2&list=PLltxIX4B8_URNUzDE2sXctnUAEXgEDDGn

Update

Fall 2022

In Canada, the provincial, federal government and the media are pushing the vaccine and the mask narrative. There is a public inquiry into the Freedom Convoy emergency measures. It is only an inquiry. Do not expect more out of it as long as the media control the narrative.

The government continue with their objective to establish a one world in dis-order.

The woke are gaining increased influence over our children, leaving parent frustrated and silence, afraid that if they speak out their children will be taking away.

Resent update on doctors death rate in Canada

Dr. William Makis 93 Dead Doctors After Vaccine Rollout

https://rumble.com/embed/v1spu0s/?pub=gi6jj

Very Disturbing to watch

Disturbing 'Died Suddenly' Content - 'Doctors Baffled By Increase In Sudden Adult Death Syndrome'

https://rumble.com/embed/v1sks4q/?pub=gi6jj

It is difficult to get accurate information in Canada. Alberta is the only one open to share some information

Unprecedented Rise in Deaths from 'Unknown Causes' Becomes Leading Killer in 2020 and 2021 https://adversereactionreport.com/reactions/alberta-canada-unprecedented-rise-in-deaths-from-unknown-causes-becomes-leading-killer-in-2020-and-2021/

'Unknown Cause' Is the Top Cause of Death in Canada! https://www.globalresearch.ca/unknown-cause-top-cause-death-canada/5791610

There are reports of serious injuries and death among the vaccinated. Peter McCullough, MD, MPH speaks about his concern about covid-19 vaccine https://rumble.com/vnbv86-winning-the-war-against-therapeutic-nihilism-and-trusted-treatments-vs-unte.html

Dr. Mike Yeadon: They Lied About Everything, Including That There Was a Pandemic https://rumble.com/v1qztky-dr.-mike-yeadon-they-lied-about-everything-including-that-there-was-a-pande.html

Canada Covid-19 statistic   https://www.jccf.ca/covid-stats/

The sad state of the US department of Defence, is it a reflection to Canadian National defence?
https://rumble.com/embed/v1tcam6/?pub=gi6jj

Canada stillbirth rate, 'This is Horrifying': Dr. James Thorp Has Seen 'Death and Destruction' Like Never Before https://rumble.com/embed/v1tqd50/?pub=gi6jj

For centuries, the global elite have broadcast their intentions to depopulate the world - even to the point of carving them into stone. And yet… we never seem to believe them. Stew Peters Network

World Premiere: Died Suddenly https://rumble.com/embed/v1to6s2/?pub=gi6jj

www.ingramcontent.com/pod-product-compliance
Lightning Source LLC
LaVergne TN
LVHW050023080526
838202LV00069B/6898